# AWAKENED TO A CALLING

# Awakened to a Calling

## Reflections on the Vocation of Ministry

EDITED BY ANN M. SVENNUNGSEN AND MELISSA WIGINTON

Abingdon Press
*Nashville*

AWAKENED TO A CALLING
REFLECTIONS ON THE VOCATION OF MINISTRY

*Copyright © 2005 by Abingdon Press*

All rights reserved.

*This book is printed on acid-free paper.*

**Library of Congress Cataloging-in-Publication Data**

Awakened to a calling : reflections on the vocation of ministry / Ann M. Svennungsen and Melissa Wiginton, edtors.
     p. cm.
  Includes bibliographical references.
  ISBN 0-687-05390-0 (alk. paper)
     1. Clergy—Appointment, call, and election.   2. Vocation, Ecclesiastical.   3. Pastoral theology.
I. Svennungsen, Ann M., 1955-   II. Wiginton, Melissa, 1958-

  BV4011.4.A93 2005
  248.8'92—dc22                                                                    2004020401

05 06 07 08 09 10 11 12 13 14—10 9 8 7 6 5 4 3 2

MANUFACTURED IN THE UNITED STATES OF AMERICA

*To James L. Waits and his unfailing love for the church*

# Contents

# FOREWORD

This collection of sermons from some of America's most eminent preachers is a most fitting tribute to Jim Waits as he retires from the Fund for Theological Education. Just as they express the passion and commitment of the call to the ministry at its finest, so they portray the kind of ministry Jim Waits has embodied and sought to engender throughout his life.

It was that winsome personification of ministry that drew me to him decades ago. He had recently joined the staff of West End United Methodist Church in Nashville, and I was a junior faculty member at Vanderbilt Divinity School. I was hardly unique in my appreciation of him. It was apparent to all that he represented the best in ministry: a personal commitment that joins unself-conscious piety with social passion; character that invites implicit trust yet is seasoned with sparkling wit; an aspiration for the highest standards in ministry coupled with an unwavering determination that they should pervade the church. Early on, Jim had a vision of what the church and its ministry ought to be.

When I was invited to come to Candler School of Theology at Emory as dean in 1969, it was natural—and providential—that I would turn to him to be my closest colleague. Taking over as dean himself in 1977, Jim's wonderfully discerning eye identified outstanding new faculty, launched imaginative new programs, and developed new concepts of ministry. During that period Candler emerged as one of the nation's premier centers for ministerial education.

1

In addition to his genius for building a great faculty and inspiring a better qualified ministry, he was an ardent advocate for a more inclusive one. His early years in Mississippi had given him a passion for all who were underrepresented. For him, commitment to social justice is an expression of heartfelt conviction, not a bow to political correctness. As a result, his prophetic witness through the years has been all the more powerful.

Jim Waits has also been a strong proponent of religion and the arts. When Cannon Chapel was being designed at Emory, it was his vision to make it a center for drama, music, and the arts, as well as worship. He envisioned its role on campus to be not unlike that of the cathedrals of old, the center of life in all of its fullness where the community could find its voice and express its highest aspirations.

Jim has shown himself to be a superb administrator in his various roles. For him the executive office is itself an aspect of ministry where, in exercising fairness and inclusion, one engenders mutual confidence. His restraint in the use of power and his resistance to its blandishments have given him enormous moral authority. In his hands administration becomes transformed into spiritual leadership.

It was recognition of these gifts and appreciation of his rich experience that brought him to the presidency of the Association of Theological Schools (ATS) in North America. Having been an outstanding success as dean, he now had an opportunity to shape theological education at large. Under his leadership ATS pursued excellence in a most determined way, establishing the first zero-based accrediting standards since the 1930s. During his tenure there was a dramatic increase in the number of schools linked to the accrediting organization, reflecting both the new importance of ATS and a concerted effort to assist smaller schools in becoming eligible for membership. He infused new energy and purpose into the association, reinvented and retooled many of its activities, and established seminars for presidential leadership.

Drawing upon his own catholic view of the church and its ministry, where the world is seen as the church's parish (to paraphrase Wesley), he led the development of programs of theology and the arts and made them accessible to all seminaries, not just a select few.

It was at the height of a most successful tenure at ATS that he chose to become president of the Fund for Theological Education (FTE). At first glance it seemed an unpropitious move. The FTE had become virtually moribund from its glory years of the Rockefeller Trial Year Fellowships and the Benjamin Mays Fellowships. Once the funding for these innovative programs ran out, it had become increasingly difficult to obtain dependable support.

It was the Fund, with its bright past but uncertain future, that Jim Waits felt called to revive. He was intrigued by the possibilities of addressing creatively the enormous need in the church for fresh, talented, and diverse leaders.

FTE proved a perfect venue for Jim Waits. His new vocation was to see that the call to ministry broke through the cliché-ridden patterns of conventional religious life so that it could be heard, and heeded, by a broader and more diverse segment of the younger generation. He was convinced that the church itself had a calling to deal with the world in all its complexities and needs—that the institutional church was itself not the object of ministry but the vehicle for ministry to the world. To accomplish this demanding understanding of mission and ministry required the best mentors for the ablest candidates.

This vision of what ministry could be attracted a strong new board, an energized staff, and ultimately substantial backing, including many local congregations as well as foundations. One can hardly overstate the transformation he achieved. It was based on his conviction that the ministry is the most challenging and needed of all the professions; that too often the role of the minister is seen as institutional caretaker, not the enabler of the laity in addressing issues of moment beyond the church; and that if persons are presented with such a compelling vision of the ministry, they will respond. Further, if congregations are invited to back such programs they will come through. Under Jim Waits's leadership, they have.

Specifically, the FTE inaugurated the Partnership for Excellence, a program linking congregations, colleges, and seminaries in enlisting promising students for the ministry. Further, it initiated the Expanding Horizons partnerships, designed to attract and support African American doctoral students in their advanced religious studies. Through these programs FTE has breathed fresh life into our understanding of the vocation of ministry and provided new means to support preparation for it at all levels.

If one were to characterize Jim Waits it would be as senior statesman of theological education. This is because of his passion for excellence, his commitment to diversity and justice, his profound appreciation of vocation, and his remarkable administrative gifts. He has brought wise judgment and implicit trust to all his endeavors. He has made theological education exciting, deserving of broad interest and genuine respect. He has shown that the calling to the ministry is a challenge worthy of the very best. His own ministry exemplifies this.

As he retires, he leaves behind a revitalized and greatly strengthened Fund for Theological Education, one fully capable of carrying on the highest standards of ministerial preparation and vocation. For that we—and the church—are deeply in his debt.

James T. Laney

# Introduction

Each of us holds within our souls the hope for something more—something more than what we experience, accomplish, and consume. Sometimes that hope grows into longing for a life that brings together our dreams, our gifts, our wounds, and our truest loves. That longing is what pulls each of us toward vocation. If you feel that longing, be it a mild tingle or a sweet pain, then this book is for you.

The writers of these reflections preached them first as sermons to particular groups of young adults who were wondering whether, or in what ways, they were called to ministry. If you are searching for your vocation, you may be looking, listening, and waiting for something in the same way those who first heard these sermons preached were looking, listening, and waiting for something to answer whether and how they were called to use their life's energy and gifts. The hearers were listening for the sound of a certain something—the soft, sure click of the right key finally fitting into a door straining to be opened, the satisfying click that one feels as relief, a click that is the kind of knowing captured in T. S. Eliot's words: "The end of our exploring shall be to arrive where we started and know the place for the first time." Coming to one's vocation can feel a lot like opening the door to home. So, as you read these essays, pay attention. Shake yourself wide-awake. Notice when your heart starts racing or your throat tightens or you tear up or you feel angry, scared, or excited. Your body, heart, and mind all hold clues to the way home, so make a point to take in the information they provide. The writers of these essays do not use words carelessly; they stake their claim on the power of words, so become acutely aware of how the words move powerfully in you.

Our relief at the click of a key that fits—that knowing that comes by receiving powerful words—opens up new possibilities, even as that knowing may come and go. T. S. Eliot began the above sentence whose end is quoted above by saying, "We shall not cease from exploration. . . ." We nudge the door open to peek behind cupboard doors and poke around the nooks and crannies of this place that feels like it might be home, might be our vocation. You may know immediately how all the pieces of your life should now be arranged. Or you may be settling in one evening only to wake up the next morning convinced that this place—this work or way of being—is not where you belong at all. So read this book slowly. And do more than pay attention to the power of words. Use this book as a wake-up call for taking the time to try something and to look around. Give yourself time to take what you discover beyond your cozy reading spot. Spend a year in a volunteer service program. Do an internship in a congregation, an institution, or an organization dedicated to what you long to do. Pray. Meet with a spiritual director. And look around: you happen to be exploring vocation at a time when many people and institutions aim to support young people doing just that. Many theology schools have opportunities for high school students to delve into the question of vocation as part of Christian discipleship. (You can find them listed on www.thefund.org.) Many colleges intentionally address the theological exploration of vocation. (Visit www.ptev.org for a list.) Several Web sites point you toward books about vocation, internships, and other kinds of exploratory adventures, ask good questions and give helpful information: among them are www.isgodcallingyou.org, www.heargodscall.org, www.exploreministry.org, www.united-church.ca/ministry/becoming, www.elca.org/dm/candidacy/explore.html, www.askthequestion.org and www.theplse.org.

As Christians, we know this business of finding vocation— this business of becoming fully human in relationship with

God—as both existential and communal work. You may have noticed that T. S. Eliot did not say, "I shall not cease from exploring"; he said rather, "We shall not cease from exploration and the end of our exploring shall be to arrive where we started and know the place for the first time." After you read this book by yourself, get together with one or two other people who long for more than what we can experience, accomplish, and consume and read these essays out loud to each other. Speak and hear them in community. Talk to people about what exhilarates, confuses, or scares you. Tell your pastor, your grandmother, or your roommate, "I'm reading this book about being awakened to a calling and I really think I might be called to become a minister (or a teacher or a chef or a CEO)" and listen to what they say. Do not be surprised to hear, "Of course. I knew that." Or, they might say, "I never would have imagined that. Tell me about it." Settling into that vocational space that may be home, you will likely discover that other people also recognize it as where you belong. Some may not get it, but some people will. You do not have to go it alone.

All of the preachers who wrote these essays are friends of Jim Waits, in whose honor this book is published. Some are teachers, scholars, and administrators he hired. Some are lifelong colleagues in theological education. Some allegiances grew from shared dreams for the church. None of these people came to their vocations by themselves, nor do they live out their vocations alone. Jim, for instance, gave each of these people a place to speak and gathered listeners to receive their words. Jim has a real gift for inviting people into the places where they belong, where they awaken to their vocations. This book extends that gift on your behalf. Pay attention as you read. Take time to look around and try some things to move into your call. Invite other people to explore with you and beckon other people into their own vocational homes. Awaken to your calling.

Melissa Wiginton

# Contributors

## The Fund for Theological Education

The Fund for Theological Education (FTE) is the nation's leading advocate for excellence and diversity in Christian ministry. FTE provides fellowships and a network of support to the next generation of leaders among pastors and scholars—gifted young people called from all denominations and racial ethnic backgrounds. The Fund is also a resource for educational and faith communities, offering programs that encourage high-quality candidates to explore vocations in ministry and teaching. Since 1954, the Atlanta-based Fund has awarded more than 5,500 fellowships in partnership with others committed to the future of quality leadership for the church.

## Brad R. Braxton, Ph.D.

Brad R. Braxton is Associate Professor of Homiletics and New Testament at Vanderbilt Divinity School in Nashville, Tennessee. Prior to joining the Vanderbilt faculty, he taught at Wake Forest University Divinity School in Winston-Salem, North Carolina. Braxton earned a B.A. from the University of Virginia, a Master of Philosophy in New Testament studies from the University of Oxford, and a Ph.D. in New Testament studies from Emory University. He is the author of three books: *The Tyranny of Resolution: I Corinthians 7:17-24* (Society of Biblical Literature, 2000); *No Longer Slaves: Galatians and African American Experience* (The Liturgical Press, 2002); and *Preaching Paul* (Abingdon Press, 2004). Braxton, an ordained Baptist minister, served for five years as the Senior Pastor of the Douglas Memorial Community Church, a six hundred member interdenominational congregation in Baltimore, Maryland.

## Walter Brueggemann, Ph.D.

Walter Brueggemann is the William Marcellus McPheeters Emeritus Professor of Old Testament at Columbia Theological Seminary. He is an ordained minister in the United Church of Christ and has recently published *An Introduction to the Old Testament: The Canon and Christian Imagination* (Louisville: Westminster John Knox Press, 2003) and *Inscribing the Text: Sermons and Prayers of Walter Brueggemann*, ed. Anna Carter Florence (Minneapolis: Fortress Press, 2004).

## Fred Craddock, Ph.D.

Fred Craddock is founding pastor and Pastor Emeritus of Cherry Log Christian (Disciples of Christ) Church, in Cherry Log, Georgia. Dr. Craddock received his Master of Divinity degree from Phillips Theological Seminary in Oklahoma and earned his Ph.D. in New Testament at Vanderbilt University. He was awarded the Darbeth Distinguished Professor of Preaching and New Testament while teaching at Phillips, and similarly received the Bandy Distinguished Professor of Preaching and New Testament Chair in his time teaching at Candler School of Theology under the deanship of James L.

Waits. Dr. Craddock was named by *Time* magazine as one of the ten best preachers in America. He is the author of numerous books and collections of sermons. He and his preaching are dearly loved by countless pastors and Christians across the country.

## James T. Laney, Ph.D.

James T. Laney has had a career as minister, educator, and ambassador. Most recently, as U.S. Ambassador to South Korea (1993–1997), he was credited with playing a key role in defusing the 1994 nuclear crisis with North Korea. Prior to his ambassadorship, Dr. Laney served as president of Emory University for sixteen years. Under his leadership Emory came to be ranked in the top tier of American universities, and the endowment grew tenfold, to sixth among all colleges. He also served as dean of Candler School of Theology (1969–1977) and taught at Vanderbilt and Harvard. Dr. Laney has served also as pastor and with his wife, Berta Radford Laney, as a missionary in South Korea. He was educated at Yale (B.A., M.Div., Ph.D.). Dr. Laney continues to be engaged in the Korean situation, serving as co-chair of the Council on Foreign Relations Task Force on Korea, making frequent trips to Asia in private and official capacities. He currently chairs the United Board for Christian Higher Education in Asia, is a trustee of the Henry Luce Foundation, and chairs the Faith And The City program in Atlanta with Andrew Young.

## Thomas G. Long, Ph.D.

Thomas G. Long is the Bandy Professor of Preaching at Candler School of Theology. He has also taught at Columbia Theological Seminary and Princeton Theological Seminary and has also served as Director of Congregational Resources and Geneva Press for the Presbyterian Publishing Corporation. He is a graduate of Erskine Theological Seminary and Princeton Theological Seminary. The author of several books, including *The Witness of Preaching* (Louisville: Westminster John Knox Press, 1990), *Preaching and the Literary Forms of the Bible* (Minneapolis: Augsburg Fortress Publishers, 1989), *Whispering the Lyrics* (Lima, Ohio: CSS Publishing, 1995), *Beyond the Worship Wars* (Bethesda: Alban Institute, 2001), and commentaries on Matthew and Hebrews, Dr. Long engages in an active ministry of preaching and lecturing.

## Ellen Echols Purdum, M.Div.

Ellen Echols Purdum holds an M.Div. degree from the Candler School of Theology and recently completed a year of Anglican Studies at the General Theological Seminary in New York City in preparation for ordination to the priesthood in the Episcopal Church. She is a Phi Beta Kappa graduate of Emory University with a B.A. in English and formerly was a high school teacher at the Westminster Schools in Atlanta, Georgia. At Westminster Ms. Purdum received the Merrill Award for Excellence in Teaching in recognition of work teaching freshman and senior English courses and developing and teaching interdisciplinary and service-learning electives for seniors in partnership with other agencies and educational institutions. A parishioner at St. Luke's Episcopal Church and an Associate at the Green Bough House of Prayer, a retreat center in south Georgia, Ms. Purdum has accepted a call to St. Anne's Episcopal Church in Atlanta as an assistant priest. Ms. Purdum served on the staff of the Fund for Theological Education from 1999 until 2003 as Assistant to the President, James L. Waits.

# Ann M. Svennungsen, M.Div.

Ann M. Svennungsen is president of The Fund for Theological Education. She graduated summa cum laude with a degree in Mathematics from Concordia College in Minnesota. In 1981, she received her M.Div. from Luther Seminary, where she was a recipient of the Seminary Preaching Award. In 1996, having served pastorates in Iowa City and Minneapolis, Pastor Svennungsen was called as senior pastor of Trinity Lutheran Church, a 3,700-member congregation in Moorhead, Minnesota and the largest ELCA congregation to be led by a woman senior pastor. The Reverend Svennungsen has given commencement addresses at Concordia College and Luther Seminary, preached at the ELCA Churchwide Assembly, presented a 2004 Earl Lecture at Pacific School of Religion, and published several articles and Bible studies. Currently, she serves on the Alban Institute Board of Trustees and the Presidential Search Committee at Pacific Lutheran Theological Seminary.

# Barbara Brown Taylor, M.Div.

Barbara Brown Taylor is an Episcopal priest who teaches religion at Piedmont College in Demorest, Georgia. Before becoming a full-time teacher in 1997, she spent fifteen years in parish ministry. In 2001, she joined the faculty of Columbia Theological Seminary in Decatur, Georgia, as adjunct professor of Christian spirituality. An editor-at-large for *The Christian Century* and sometime commentator on Georgia Public Radio, she is the author of ten books, including *When God Is Silent* (Cowley Publications, 1998), *God in Pain: Teaching Sermons on Suffering* (Abingdon Press, 1998), and *Speaking of Sin: The Lost Language of Salvation* (Cowley Publications, 2000).

# Melissa Wiginton, M.Div.

Melissa Wiginton is the founding director of the Partnership for Excellence of The Fund for Theological Education. She received an M.Div. summa cum laude from Candler School of Theology, where she was recognized by the Emory University President's Commission on the Status of Women for the feminist scholarship. She also earned a B.A. and J.D. from the University of Texas at Austin. Prior to entering divinity school, Ms. Wiginton spent thirteen years practicing law in Austin, Texas. She and her daughter are contributing authors of *Way to Live: Christian Practices for Teens* (Nashville: Upper Room Books, 2002).

# Jeremiah A. Wright, Jr., Ph.D.

Pastor Jeremiah A. Wright, Jr. attended Virginia Union University in Richmond, Virginia and holds master's degrees from Howard University and the University of Chicago Divinity School. His doctorate was received from the United Theological Seminary under Dr. Samuel DeWitt Proctor. Pastor Wright was called to serve the congregation of Trinity United Church of Christ in March of 1972. Trinity's membership was eighty-seven adults in that year. The membership now exceeds eight thousand. Under Pastor Wright's leadership, thirty-five seminary graduates have been ordained to the Christian ministry and twenty-nine students are presently enrolled in fully accredited seminaries, preparing themselves for full-time ministry.

# MARY AND MARTHA AND THE MYERS-BRIGGS

## Ellen Echols Purdum

> *Now as they went on their way, he entered a certain village, where a woman named Martha welcomed him into her home. She had a sister named Mary, who sat at the Lord's feet and listened to what he was saying. But Martha was distracted by her many tasks; so she came to him and asked, "Lord, do you not care that my sister has left me to do all the work by myself? Tell her then to help me." But the Lord answered her, "Martha, Martha, you are worried and distracted by many things; there is need of only one thing. Mary has chosen the better part, which will not be taken away from her."* —Luke 10:38-42

I am Martha. I am a person who is task-oriented, always anticipating what needs to be accomplished. I am good with details, and my gifts include planning and organizing. While I have lived long enough to know that much of life is messy, it is a challenge for me to bless it that way. My preference is to make lists in which the items are arranged both by category and by priority, which is another way of saying I like structure and order. I especially enjoy the satisfaction of checking off the items on my list. Because I am a Martha and always thinking ahead about the logistics, my to-do list never seems to get any shorter. My husband will tell you that task completion is a live issue around our house.

I am dependable, hardworking, responsible, and efficient. And though I hate admitting it, I am fueled by anxiety and talk about it a lot.

I also am a Mary. This was a fairly recent revelation. I am a person who needs solitude and silence with a palpability I can feel in my very skin and muscles and bones. I like to read and to think and to write, and I go on retreats in order to be by myself, to be quiet, to reflect and to pray, and blessedly, to permit other people to deal with the logistics. Coming to this realization later rather than earlier in life has meant that my own journey of vocational discernment for the priesthood has been long, one in which I took some exits too early and some too late, stopping at green lights and accelerating through stop signs. And while I take seriously the counsel of a wise friend who pointed out that I still would have everything in the trunk of my car when I rounded another turn, that no experience ever is wasted, I am acutely aware that not recognizing I am both a Martha and a Mary has made the journey difficult.

This recent knowledge about myself, that I am a Mary as well as a Martha, has been confirmed with particular force during the last several weeks. I am spending the summer fulfilling a required unit of clinical pastoral education (C.P.E.) in an urban hospital in Atlanta, one that boasts the second largest trauma center in the state. I'm not exactly sure what I had expected a summer of C.P.E. in a hospital to be like, but I suppose I thought I would be going from room to room on my assigned floor, listening a lot, spreading good cheer if I could, handing out little copies of the New Testament with the Psalms attached, and in some occasional, valley-of-the-shadow hours, hoping to bring comfort to the dying and to their families. That, and sitting in a group with other aspiring ministers, talking about how the results of our personality inventory tests have influenced our pastoral identities.

I have done some of those things, but much of my time has been spent in the trauma bay of the emergency room, where chaplains in this particular hospital are expected to participate in what is known as the interdisciplinary response team. When the whirr of the Life Flight helicopter can be heard approaching, the pager goes off, and the overhead speakers sound Trauma I Alert, I know I have somewhere between four and eight minutes to get to the emergency room, don gown, mask, and gloves, and gather all the paperwork I will need to fill out when the patient arrives. Once the pilot and medic burst through the door with the gurney, the scene becomes chaotic, despite the fact that, in theory at least, everyone has a clearly assigned role. Part of my job is to start listening to the barrage of shouts and begin writing down information as fast as I can: John Doe, forty to fifty years old, MVA, entrapment, no restraint, length of extrication thirty minutes, multiple fractures left femur, collapsed lung, Hispanic, call the translator, no ID. Another part of my job involves collecting the bloody remnants of clothing being cut off by the medical staff and going through them to find something, anything, to help me notify the family. Often the doctor will toss me a gold wedding ring or a silver cross over his or her shoulder. A pen, a pack of cigarettes, an Our Lady of Guadalupe icon that attaches to a windshield, a wallet if I'm lucky—I put them all in an envelope or a bag, label everything three times, and take them to the security office. Eventually I will find myself sitting with a distraught family, saying a prayer if they want one, getting them cold water if they don't, relaying what little information the doctor will give me, but that comes later.

This past Monday I served my first twenty-four-hour on-call shift. During the night I responded to five trauma alerts, three of them back to back. Car wreck, car wreck, four-wheeler rollover, motorcycle crash, car wreck. Closed head wounds, internal injuries, one dead infant. For close to twelve hours I am mostly Martha, fulfilling my duties in the trauma bay, contacting parents and spouses, escorting families from the emergency room to the OR, to the intensive care unit, arranging meetings with the surgeons, helping people find bathrooms, the coffee machine, the water fountain, waking up the Catholic priest a wife has asked me to call, instructing people to turn off their cellular phones. By 3:00 A.M. close to one hundred people have filled the ICU waiting area to overflowing. By 5:30 A.M. things are beginning to quiet down, and I take the elevator up to the fifth floor, where the chaplain's so-called sleeping room commands an impressive view of dawn breaking over the downtown skyline.

I think that surely the on-call tasks are over for the night, at least until the rush hour traffic starts to move, so I take off my shoes, remove the pager from my belt, and stretch out on the bed, hoping for some rest, if not actual sleep. When the pager goes off at 6:07, the illuminated message reads not trauma alert, but code 99, which means that somewhere in the hospital somebody's heart or breathing has stopped. I pull my shoes back on and hurriedly find my way to the nursing station of the fourth floor, where eight or ten medical staff have crowded into room 449 to try to revive the patient who has coded. A nurse points to a young man sitting alone in the hallway, wrapped in a hospital blanket and weeping. I pull up a chair next to him, put my arm around his shoulders, and ask him his name and who it is in the room. "My best friend," he tells me. I continue to sit with him, get him some coffee, and try to learn something about his best friend. I do not learn much, except that he is twenty-eight, that his only relative is a mother in New Jersey who cannot afford to make the trip to Atlanta, and that his friends have been taking shifts at the hospital since Saturday. One of them, a young woman, joins us in the hallway. When at last a medical resident emerges from the room and walks over to us, we know from the closed expression on his face that they have been unsuccessful. The two young people cling to each other, oddly quiet now, and I ask them gently if they would like to see their friend. This question frightens them, and although I reassure them that of course, they don't have to go into the room if they don't want to, they remain agitated. I leave them briefly to ask another nurse about trying to contact the mother in New Jersey, and when I return, I discover that they have fled.

Standing in the hallway outside room 449, as the crisis downshifts to routine hospital activity at 7:00 A.M., I remember that if no one comes to claim the deceased, the body will go to the morgue and then to a pauper's grave. This thought fills me with immense sadness and helplessness. I do not know what else to do, and so I do the one needful thing I can think of. I go back to the sleeping room in which I have not slept, retrieve my *Book of Common Prayer*, and return to room 449. Looking down at the face of this young man, beautiful and fine-boned, with thick dreadlocks spread across the pillow, much younger-looking than twenty-eight, I read aloud prayers from the burial service, rite one, because the words are old-fashioned and eloquent and strong. And in that moment, I know that I am mostly Mary. In that moment, despite the tears I am wiping away from under my glasses, I have the sense that "Here I am, where I ought to be."

I do not tell you this long story to scare you about C.P.E.; rather, I offer you this story because I suspect that some of you also may experience your lives both as Marthas and as Marys. I suspect you would not be considering or preparing for pastoral ministry as your life's work if you did not. My hunch is that in your own journeys of vocational discernment, you have wondered about, and even wrestled with, what the Trappist monk Thomas Merton referred to as a calling to both an active and a contemplative life.

The Presbyterian minister and author Frederick Buechner, who was, by the way, one of the first four FTE Fellows back in 1954, frames the notion of vocation a bit differently. He writes in his book *Wishful Thinking: A Theological ABC*: "The place God calls you to is the place where your deep gladness and the world's deep hunger meet."[1] Some of you may be familiar with Buechner's description of calling; it has become well known, well used, and often misquoted among people who care about such things. And while any catchy quotation may run the risk of becoming overused and trite, I find that Buechner's description still catches me, someone who has struggled with being both a Martha and a Mary. It catches me because I know that as a Martha, I have been distracted by my many tasks in trying to address the world's needs, deep or otherwise. You will notice that I have already misquoted Buechner; he says the world's deep hunger, not the world's deep needs. For the moment, though, I am going to let that misquotation stand and suggest that it's the Martha in me who hears it that way.

The part of the quotation that still catches me is that business about one's deep gladness, the part that is supposed to meet the world's deep needs and result in the recognition of one's vocation. It sounds so simple, even mathematical: $V = X + Y$. Just figure out what the two parts are, and voilà, there is one's calling. Unfortunately, though, while some annoying few among us always have known what they wanted to be when they grew up, for many of us, that mathematical equation resists resolution.

I do not think this is because we are unaware of the world's deep needs. At some level, anybody who turns on CNN or listens to National Public Radio or reads the front page of the daily paper is aware of the deep needs of the world. Many have come this far in your vocational journeys precisely because you are aware of, and have responded to, the deep needs of the world. You have ladled soup in homeless shelters, you have gone on mission trips to Central America, you have built Habitat houses, you have protested for peace, you have counseled battered women, you have tutored or led Vacation Bible School for children who, most assuredly, have been left behind. I am not trying to suggest that these deep needs are not complex; most of them are. What I am trying to suggest is that recognizing them may be easier than recognizing one's own deep gladness.

That may sound crazy to you, but it does not seem crazy to me. When as a college student at Emory I visited the career center, the counselor kept asking me, "What is it that you really like to do?" "I don't know, I don't know, I don't know," I would respond, feeling somehow pigeonholed and panicky. When I have taken the Myers-Briggs and the Enneagram personality inventory tests, and have had to choose between whether I would rather sit by myself on a rock by a stream or go to a party, I have been known to furiously scribble in both answers with my number 2 pencil, drawing a thick black arrow to connect the two. "Both, both," I have thought to myself, "I would rather do both of them!" When I was in seminary and struggling with the question of ordination, I went from person to person to person, asking, "How do you know? How do you know? How do you know?" Most of the answers I received were well intended, but not helpful, at least at the time. "I just know." Oh, wonderful. "God told me." Well, bully for you, I guess God doesn't speak to me. And this, from a theology professor, "It's ontological." Please.

Why is it so difficult to be in touch with what makes one deeply glad? How hard can it be to have the sense of "Here I am, where I ought to be"? I could say to you, well, it's different for every person, but since that response might wind up sounding equally well intended but unhelpful, I am going to propose a couple of possibilities. The first one has to do with our families of origin, the ways in which we take on roles, develop personality traits, and seek to fulfill expectations as part of the dynamics of how our families operate. In my own family, the operative message was very clear: do something practical so that you always will be warm and safe and dry. In and of itself, there's certainly nothing wrong with being warm and safe and dry; just ask any homeless person on the streets about that. The problem comes, I believe, when one spends so much time and energy trying to secure warmth and safety and dryness that one ceases to hear the longings of one's own heart. We find ourselves not living our own lives and become, instead, what a friend refers to as "our parents' projects."

But if some of us are fortunate enough to have parents who encourage us to follow the longings of our hearts, even to places that are not guaranteed to keep us warm and safe and dry, the culture in which we live also offers myriad opportunities for that deep gladness to be obscured, or worse, eroded altogether. The pace at which we live, driven by the tyranny of technology, does not invite reflection, does not offer us a "time-out" to feel our own feelings or think our own thoughts or register our own resistances. The media, marketers, and advertisers, who are more than willing to drown out any inklings of genuine deep gladness we sense and tell us what that deep gladness should be about, are more than willing to ensure that our lives are constructed externally, rather than birthed from the inside out.

Madeleine Hutin, a Frenchwoman who founded the Order of the Little Sisters of Jesus in 1939 in Algiers, has something to say about this. Striving to live out an intense commitment to contemplative prayer as well as a commitment to enter fully into the lives and culture of her poor neighbors in tiny villages across North Africa, Little Sister Madeleine, as she became, noted that "the world looks for efficiency more than for the unobtrusiveness of the hidden life."[2] Given the kind of order that she founded, Little Sister Madeleine may herself have been both a Martha and a Mary. I feel sure she performed many tasks in response to the deep needs of the community in which she lived and served. But what Little Sister Madeleine seems to have understood so clearly was the danger of letting the hidden life, wherein resides one's deep gladness, remain unrecognized and untended, in one's anxious and distracted drive to be efficient, to be productive, to complete the tasks deemed necessary.

Jesus puts his finger right on it, of course. In the Gospel story, which at first glance appears to pit two sisters against each other, the problem is not that Martha has the wrong gifts for ministry and that Mary has the right ones. The problem is not that Mary wins the prize for being the real disciple and that Martha loses. This is not a contest. Frankly, I don't believe Jesus gives a hoot that Martha is an ESTJ on the Myers-Briggs and that Mary is an INFP. When he says that Mary has chosen the better part, I think it's important not to get so stuck on the word "better" that we ignore the word "part." In ministry there are many parts, after all. And the Greek also is instructive: it's not "better part," it's "good part."

No, what Jesus puts his finger on with Martha and her many tasks is the fact that something has obscured, or even eroded, what is the good part. Something has caused her not to recognize and live out of her own particular deep gladness. "Martha, Martha," he says, "you are worried and distracted by many things; there is need of only one thing."

Speaking as a Martha, this response hits home. I hate it that it hits home. My dependable, hard-working, responsible, and efficient self wants to shake my to-do list in Jesus' face and shout, "What do you mean, only one thing? Look at this list, look at all these deep needs of the world! How do you expect me to meet them sitting around like my woolgathering sister over there? Get with the program, Jesus!" Remember, I am a person who is fueled by anxiety and talks about it a lot. But remember, too, that I also am a Mary who only recently has realized that she even has a hidden life, and that she needs to put down that to-do list, close her ears to the constant chatter of familial and cultural pressures and expectations, and sit at the feet of Jesus in order for that deep gladness to be nurtured. Not to worry, that list will still be there when she returns. The deep needs of the world always will be waiting for us to attend to, both as Marthas and as Marys.

Don't worry about what you score on personal inventory tests: some of us are introverts, some of us are extroverts; some of us love to think, some of us love to help; some of us dream, some of us make do-to lists; some of us are organized, some of us are, well, not. All of these particularities matter because they are part of us. But none of them is really the reason that we have the potential to become faithful ministers. The real reason is that somewhere inside of us lies a deep spring of gladness of which we are becoming aware. You may have experienced this deep gladness as a ripple, or as a sudden, overflowing gush, or as a slow and steady drip, or even as one single, cool drop. However you are beginning to experience it, you know how it makes you feel, and it's the opposite of anxious and distracted. It feels life-giving and liberating.

Pay attention to those ripples and gushes, drips and drops. Trust them and follow them. See where they take you. Pay just as much attention to those moments when you are feeling anxious and distracted. Try to see what it is that's obscuring, even eroding, that deep gladness. Put down that list and start instead with those ripples and gushes, drips and drops. The deep needs of the world will make themselves apparent soon enough, and the convergence Buechner speaks of will happen. Jesus reminds us of one other thing in the story of Martha and Mary in Luke's Gospel, and that is that you have a choice. The tyrants of anxiety and distraction may try to convince you otherwise, but don't believe them. Believe that there is only one needful thing and that it will not be taken away from you.

# Notes

1. Frederick Buechner, *Wishful Thinking: A Theological ABC* (New York: Harper & Row, 1973), p. 95.

2. Robert Ellsberg, *All Saints: Daily Reflections on Saints, Prophets, and Witnesses for Our Time* (New York: Crossroads Publishing, 1997), p. 484.

# If Only I Could Be Sure

## Fred Craddock

*When Saul saw the army of the Philistines, he was afraid, and his heart trembled greatly. When Saul inquired of the LORD, the LORD did not answer him, not by dreams, or by Urim, or by prophets. Then Saul said to his servants, "Seek out for me a woman who is a medium, so that I may go to her and inquire of her." His servants said to him, "There is a medium at Endor." So Saul disguised himself and put on other clothes and went there, he and two men with him. They came to the woman by night. And he said, "Consult a spirit for me, and bring up for me the one whom I name to you." The woman said to him, "Surely you know what Saul has done, how he has cut off the mediums and the wizards from the land. Why then are you laying a snare for my life to bring about my death?" But Saul swore to her by the LORD, "As the LORD lives, no punishment shall come upon you for this thing."*
—1 Samuel 28:5-10

*One day, as we were going to the place of prayer, we met a slave girl who had a spirit of divination and brought her owners a great deal of money by fortune-telling. While she followed Paul and us, she would cry out, "These men are slaves of the Most High God, who proclaim to you a way of salvation." She kept doing this for many days. But Paul, very much annoyed, turned and said to the spirit, "I order you in the name of Jesus Christ to come out of her." And it came out that very hour. But when her owners saw that their hope of making money was gone, they seized Paul and Silas and dragged them into the marketplace before the authorities.*

—Acts 16:16-19

*I am speaking the truth in Christ—I am not lying; my conscience confirms it by the Holy Spirit—I have great sorrow and unceasing anguish in my heart. For I could wish that I myself were accursed and cut off from Christ for the sake of my own people, my kindred according to the flesh. They are Israelites, and to them belong the adoption, the glory, the covenants, the giving of the law, the worship, and the promises; to them belong the patriarchs, and from them, according to the flesh, comes the Messiah, who is over all, God blessed forever. Amen.* —Romans 9:1-5

"The Art of Ministry"—not too many years ago a title like that would not fly in America. It would not fly, because ministry was suspicious of art. Art had nothing to do with ministry. Ministry regarded art as just an abbreviation of artificial. That which is honest and true and worthy of good consideration is not heartfelt, it's straightforward, sometimes crude and never pleasant. But art—art is bought, it's whipped cream, it's optional, it's a flourish, it does nothing for anybody, actually. It's the curl of carrots on the side of the plate. It's the little sprig—what is that green stuff? Parsley, yes. It's the little sprig of parsley, but it is not the meat and potatoes at all. Arthur Schlesinger, Jr. says there is a mainstream in the middle of American history that he calls anti-intellectual. I think it would be better to say anticultural: the suspicion of that which is well done. If you show signs of having rehearsed and having prepared, then obviously it is not of God. I went to seminary with that conviction, and in the class of Public Worship, Dr. Osmond said,

"You will, on Friday, turn in your prayers," and I said, "How do you turn in a prayer?" "Well, you write out the prayers and turn them in." I went to his office and made an appointment. Writing a prayer—give me a break here! Those were my camel's hair and leather girdle days, and I didn't really see much point in polishing up. And most of America, I think, was with me.

If you are well groomed, there is something suspicious about you. If you are well prepared, then what you do is pull your shirttail out and saunter about and don't look prepared. Now that is really genuine. If you read a book that's interesting, it cannot be true—it's interesting. Something as high as ministry and something as clever as art did not get along too well. It was believed that art was for the elite, the few. Those who had the leisure and the money could indulge in art and the rest of us labored in the fields of God—somewhat crude and with mud on our shoes, but honest and on-target. That was fairly commonly believed, and still believed in many places. I think it is at the heart of much of the "come as you are" movement in the church, and the minister does not realize how long it takes in front of the mirror to look casual. We know better now that it is not true that there is no empathy between art and ministry.

But what is art, anyway? It is a meaningful and often pleasing arrangement of sounds and colors and movements and shapes and actions that affect people. I asked Maya Angelou once, years ago when we were on a program together and she read some of her own poems, "Why, if you were engaged in a struggle to bring rights to black women in America, would you choose poetry, so fragile a craft as poetry, to do such a mighty battle?" She said, "Well, I've never been asked that before, but I think the truth of the matter is that the poem goes straight to the heart," and then she laughed and said, "You preach and bruise around on everybody with a broad sword if you want to." She had a point. It was believed that art was for the few—no, no, no. The poorest of the poor will have their art.

Nettie, my wife, and I passed by Shacktown—shacks of metal, shacks of cardboard, shacks outside of Cape Town, South Africa. There was nothing from nothing there, not even a blade of grass. But out in front of those shacks there was a small radio up on a rock. A girl who looked to be about five had the radio turned up and she was dancing with no reason to dance, except that you have to dance because you were created in God's image. Creation, Milton taught us, is in itself a poem. There is power in it.

The poorest of the poor live near us up in Appalachia. There are some very, very poor people. The menfolk at night will peel the plywood veneer off of a bed stand, or a head of a bed, and cut it and cut it every night after work until finally they have made a fiddle and they will play for the dance. They don't have anything except music and art. You can reduce people to the lowest of the low: put them in chains, and they will learn to drag that chain to a familiar cadence. Put them on a pile of sticks, and they will carve one into a flute. Take away all art, and they will find a way to get wild berries and draw on the face of the cave. Art is not optional, and it's not at the top. Art is where we begin. This is who we are.

Up in our area in the mountains, in the program in which I am now working, we provide music and art and storytelling for all the three- and four-year-olds in Head Start—more than four hundred children singing, playing, drawing, and remembering, and playing little instruments. And they are so poor, they are poorer than Job's turkey except for one hour each week and then they are on top of the world. That old idea of Mr. Maslow—you start with biological needs and then you go to security needs and safety needs and love needs and then when you get to the top of the pyramid there's a little music and dancing—that's just the opposite of the way it is.

We've learned about ministry as art, we just haven't learned who should be in the ministry. Should I be in the ministry? If I could only be sure of that, that is the one burning question from age eighteen until my present age of seventy-five. Have I been called into the ministry? The oldest question I guess the human race has asked of God is, "Would you show us a sign? We had it a while ago, we'll get it." God said, "Get it—I want you to lead my people." "Yes, Sir. However, I would like to be sure." A little water on the fleece and dry on the ground and so it was. And now that's good and well, should we go for two out of three?

You don't know Alex. Alex was a junior at Colorado State University with an undeclared major. You know what that is, don't you? "I don't know where in the world I am going with this stuff." Undeclared major and he was a junior already, and they were saying, "Do something!" and he said, "Okay, social studies." That was kind of a twilight zone for him. He didn't know. He was at a little church out there in Greeley, Colorado, throwing hoops with some kids about middle-school age, and their mothers had all picked them up and he was there all alone and it was getting dark out behind the church, still shooting a few hoops. "What am I going to do? Next year is my senior year. Am I going to keep doing this at the church? What am I going to do?" And he reached down and pulled up a tuft of grass and threw it up on the hood of his old car and he said to God, "If you want me to be a minister then blow that grass off my car." Later on I asked Alex, "Did God blow the grass off the car?" He said no. I said, "Then, what are you doing in the ministry if he didn't blow the grass off the car?" He said, "What kind of God would he be who would do what I've told him?" Well? And God put up with that because we want to be sure, we want to be sure.

Franz Werfel, an Austrian German, wrote a beautiful book years ago called *The Song of Bernadette*, about a Catholic girl. This was written by a Jew about a Catholic girl who had this extraordinary—she said she had an extraordinary experience of God: *The Song of Bernadette.* Mr. Werfel wrote a preface to his book, and he said, "And for the story that follows, I want you to understand that whoever wills to believe will not need final proof. For whoever does not will to believe, final proof is not enough." Well that's nice, but still if we could only be sure, if I could only be sure.

I sing with the rest of the church and I ask no dream, no prophet, no ecstasy, no sudden rending of the veil, but I don't mean it. I would like something. What I have asked for most of my life is not simply some yes from God, but a yes that is loud enough for the people around to hear it. Because I could say, "God answered my prayer," and my friends could look at each other and say, "You know, he's been that way." I would like God to answer the prayer in a voice loud enough for everybody to hear it. Confirm it.

Jesus one day, according to the Gospel of John, was standing in Jerusalem and he stopped in his teaching and looked up to heaven and said, "Father, glorify your name." And a voice from heaven said, "I have glorified it and I will glorify it again." And some standing around said, "An angel spoke" and others said, "It was thunder and I believe we are going to have a shower." Now if I had been in Jesus' place, I would have said, "God, a little louder please, so all of them will hear it." When Paul was on his way to Damascus and had that extraordinary experience of Christ, he fell to the ground. He was not alone; there were companions with him. But when it was all over, he asked his companions, "Did you see anything?" "Well, it was this bright light, but it was noon, so why not." He said, "Did you see a face?" and they said no. He said, "I saw a face and it was Jesus." Paul said, "Did you hear anything?" "Well I heard a noise or something. Why?" "Did you hear a voice? You didn't hear a voice? I heard a voice that said: 'Go into the city, I have chosen you.' Did you all hear it?" If only the others had heard it!

Why doesn't God call people into the ministry in a voice loud enough for the whole family to hear? But when I go to ordination services I can pick out the parents every time. There's that big-eyed couple, just absolutely stupid. "Is that our daughter?" "Is that our son?" "My land of living, if I could only be sure."

A whole industry, a whole industry has developed from ancient to present day to answer the question of our uncertainty, our anxiety, our not knowing. How could I be sure? It's called fortune-telling. And people have gone all over the world to get an answer.

One of the really beautiful, painfully tragic beautiful stories in the Bible is the story of King Saul at the close of 1 Samuel. Saul, tall and handsome, first King of Israel, faced the Philistine army the next day. He and his two sons were also in the military. And Saul wanted some word from God about tomorrow. It was getting late. He called in the prophets. "Is there any word from God about tomorrow?" and they said, "We haven't heard anything." He said, "Maybe I can dream the word of God" and he lay on his couch but he couldn't sleep. So he got from the temple or the tabernacle that little box of dice-like things. He shook those and tossed them to see if he could get some message, and he didn't get anything. And so finally, contrary to his own conscience and contrary to the law that he had established that banished wizards and mediums, he went to the tent of the fortune-teller at Endor. But she recognized him and she said, "What is this—a sting operation?"—something like that. He said, "Hush, woman, I have to know about tomorrow." Such a sad story, like the one presented to you from Acts 16. Paul and Silas in Philippi trying to minister and here is this fortune-telling girl. She's a slave, but the men who own her are making a lot of money because people will flock to someone who can make you sure. It feeds off of uncertainty and worry and anxiety. And when Paul cast the spirit of fortune-telling out of this slave girl, they put Paul and Silas in prison. She was a moneymaker!

Last fall I went along as a teacher of sorts with a group of twenty ministers to Greece, going to some of the places Paul had ministered and studying his letters. On the way south from Philippi we went through Delphi and the temple of Apollo. What a marvelous place, once so wealthy and such an attraction. The temple of Apollo was one of the centers of ancient Greece because Apollo gave the gift of fortune-telling. This is the way it worked: people would come to the temple and the priestess—a woman—would come out and greet them and they would give her a large sum of money and she would tell their fortune. *Will my husband be home from the war? Will my baby be born healthy? Will my ships of grain be caught in the storm on the sea? Will the army be successful in war?* Questions, questions, questions, questions. She went into a hallucinatory trance, sometimes by chewing the leaf of the laurel tree, sometimes from the fumes of lava in the rock crevices. In this state she would speak in tongues, and sometimes there was a priest there who would interpret what she said. And the people went away sure.

We spent some time, these twenty ministers and I spent some time there, and it was fascinating. Especially to hear one of the people there recite how it worked. People came, kings and peasants and everybody all over the world came to find out for sure. One of the fellows in the group, one of the ministers seemed kind of sad or down or something—melancholic. I said, "What's the matter—you didn't enjoy this?" He said, "Oh, yeah. But I was just thinking that if I had lived back then, I probably would have come here." I said, "Why?" "I would like to be sure. Am I where I am supposed to be, doing what I'm supposed to do? I would have spent all my money here." And the person who said this has been in the ministry, I would guess, twenty-five years.

If only I could be sure, is it possible to be sure? The reason I came down from the mountain is to tell you: yes, it's possible to be sure. The only way that you can be sure is that if you can hear the groan of God over what's happening to creation.

It started off as a garden. What is it now? A landfill. Violence and decay and graft and corruption and hurting and hurting and hurting and injustice and inequality, and you know God is groaning. If you are one of those chosen people who can hear the groan of God, you're in.

Years ago, I had a New Testament class. We were reading the Letter to the Romans in Greek, so you can imagine it was a small class. It was not first-year Greek; that is a pretty good size class, and second-year Greek is about half that number. Then I offered third year as an elective. We would just read and talk about Paul's letter to the Romans. Bring to class only a Greek New Testament—nothing else, no paper, and no notes, just translation—let's just read, you know. I think we were down to about six.

One of the fellows in the class—one girl and five fellows I think—one of the fellows came in a little late and already had on his tennis outfit. It was a one o'clock class. I hated one o'clock classes (and wasn't too fond of morning classes, really). But he came in all ready for tennis. Had on his little stuff with alligators on it—you know, the little shorts and the shirt matched and the socks matched and he had a can of tennis balls and his tennis racquet and New Testament and he shoved all that under his seat and opened his New Testament, and said, "Sorry I'm late." Well, I was a little aggravated. You're not supposed to come into a Greek class happy, and he obviously was happy. You were supposed to creep like a snail and in great pain and "please don't call on me"—that's the way you do it. And he came bouncing in like "tennis, anyone?" He stopped off at the Greek class on his way to the court.

So naturally I called on him, because we were in a place like Romans 9 that is tough as toenails. If you get into the third-year Greek, you stay up a little longer that night because that is tough reading. I called on him. I said, "Would you translate the first four or five verses?" So he did—beautifully. Well, I have got to do something here. I said, "Well, identify the nouns," and he identified the nouns, talked about each one of them.

You know, in the passage Paul says, "I'm telling you the truth; I'm not lying, God is my witness, my conscience is my witness, the Holy Spirit is my witness I have great sorrow—*lupae*." It is a word used to describe a woman having a baby. Hey, I have great sorrows. The words that were used to describe Jesus in Gethsemane, *lupae*, and unceasing anguish, *odunae*. Just the sound of the word in its anguish, *odunae*, is the word used to describe the rich man in torment who didn't share his food with anybody and he's in anguish. It's with this word that Paul says, "I have this sorrow, this anguish. I get up with it in the morning and go to bed with it at night, it never stops, and I could almost wish myself to be damned if it would save my people." I said to him, the student, the tennis boy, I said, "Tell me about that verb 'I could wish,' 'I could almost wish.' " He said, "Yeah, *youcoma*—that's the first singular of *youcomi*. 'I desire a wish,' but it's an unusual form." He said, "Some people call it inchoate, not imperative; some call it tangential imperfect, inchoate imperfect. It expresses something that is almost but not quite. 'I could almost wish myself to be damned for their sake.' " And Paul meant just that so I said, "Shut up." The student just translated so well.

When the class was over and he was getting his can of tennis balls and tennis racquet and was ready to go bounding to the court, I stopped him. I said, "Would you stop a minute?" He said yes. I said, "What did you think about what you read from Paul?" He said, "What?" I said, "That 'sorrow and anguish,' and 'could almost wish myself to be lost if it would save them.' " He said, "Aw Prof, I consider that really unprofessional. It's not very professional." I said, "What do you mean?" He said, "Well it's not professional to get that close to people. Pretty soon their problems are your problems. You should keep your distance from people. See ya!"

For a moment I almost envied him. I don't know if he went into ministry. You know, it's possible that he went into ministry as a professional and is still doing it as a professional. But I felt heavy about it, because if he did he would miss that almost unbearable joy of almost hearing, every once in awhile, the groan of God and trying with all your art and craft to do something about it.

# Of This Gospel...

## Thomas G. Long

*This is the reason that I Paul am a prisoner for Christ Jesus for the sake of you Gentiles—for surely you have already heard of the commission of God's grace that was given me for you, and how the mystery was made known to me by revelation, as I wrote above in a few words, a reading of which will enable you to perceive my under-standing of the mystery of Christ. In former generations this mystery was not made known to humankind, as it has now been revealed to his holy apostles and prophets by the Spirit: that is, the Gentiles have become fellow heirs, members of the same body, and sharers in the promise in Christ Jesus through the gospel.*

*Of this gospel I have become a servant according to the gift of God's grace that was given me by the working of his power. Although I am the very least of all the saints, this grace was given to me to bring to the Gentiles the news of the boundless riches of Christ, and to make every-one see what is the plan of the mystery hidden for ages in God who created all things; so that through the church the wisdom of God in its rich variety might now be made known to the rulers and authorities in the heavenly places. This was in accordance with the eternal purpose that he has carried out in Christ Jesus our Lord, in whom we have access to God in boldness and confidence through*

*faith in him. I pray therefore that you may not lose heart
over my sufferings for you; they are your glory.*
—Ephesians 3:1-13

The Letter to the Ephesians presents itself as an expression of Paul's ministry at a critical moment. What has happened is that Paul has gotten into trouble. He was always in trouble in his ministry, and now he's gotten in trouble again—bad trouble, in fact. He's been thrown in prison and this letter to the church at Ephesus is written from prison. Now, if I were in prison, writing to my home church, I would probably complain about the food, the guards, and the cramped quarters. Not Paul. He talks about the gospel, the size of the gospel. He says, "Of this gospel, I was made a minister."

There is a question that people ask ministers all the time. Even though ministers are asked this question frequently, still we never get used to it. It always catches us off guard and leaves us a little unsettled, maybe even a bit embarrassed. The question usually comes in one of those unexpected, unguarded moments. You're at a party, say, at the hors d'oeuvre table, standing there just about to slide your corn chip in the avocado dip, when somebody slips up on your blind side and says, "There's something I've been dying to ask you all evening. How *did* you happen to choose the ministry?"

Part of the awkwardness of this question is that you don't really know whether the person is expressing curiosity or sympathy. "You poor fellow, you look fairly normal. How did you happen to end up in the ministry? Did you get turned down at medical school?"

We all have our reasons, of course, why we did end up in the ministry. But that's also part of the embarrassment. You are never sure whether your story is going to live up to the expectations of the person who is asking about it. Sometimes people have a kind of *Star Wars* expectation about a call into the ministry. A white-robed figure appears in the dark with a voice like Obi-Wan Kenobi saying, "Go to seminary. The force will be with you!"

We ministers all have our experiences and stories, of course, but most of them are far less dramatic than that. How did we choose the ministry? Maybe there was a book we read, or a course we took, or a friend we had. Perhaps we had a minister we admired or we simply had a feeling in our bones. And, as a result, we chose the ministry.

But even when we've done the best we can to explain our decisions, to be clear and logical about how we chose the ministry, even when we have done all we can to tell our story—and this is the deepest embarrassment of all—we know we have not told the whole truth because there is something irrational about being in the ministry, something that will not logically compute. There is a mystery at the center of all this, and we know that when we have told people why we chose the ministry, as a matter of fact we did not choose it at all. It chose us. We were chosen for it.

You can feel Paul wrestling with this illogic in Ephesians. In fact, I defy any grammarian in the world to diagram the sentences in this passage in Ephesians. It cannot be done. The phrases and sentence fragments tumble over each other. Paul's whole statement on his ministry is an explosion of doxology. This is no logical theological treatise; it is a stammering after mystery.

You almost sense that, somewhere along the way, somebody has slipped up on Paul's blind side, and there he stands with his corn chip over the avocado dip being asked how he happened to choose the ministry. He tries on various ways of expressing it. "Well, when I thought about my vocational options..." "I took the Myers-Briggs test and it seemed to me that, um..." "When I looked at my gifts and skills and interests and career opportunities..." Finally, he simply blurts out the truth. "Of this gospel, I *was made* a minister." Something happened outside of him. Whatever was inside of him was summoned by something *outside* of him, and he was called into a place he would never have dreamed that he would have been.

A friend of mine, Don Juel, who until his untimely death taught New Testament at Princeton Theological Seminary, was a man who put his money where his mouth is. He not only taught the New Testament to seminary students, he also did Bible study with junior high students at his church. Any New Testament professor willing to work with junior highs has my deepest admiration. One Sunday afternoon Don was teaching the Gospel of Mark to the junior high group at his church, and there was one kid in the group who obviously did not want to be there. His mother had forced him to come and he resented it. You could tell it in his face. You could tell it in his body language. He turned his chair away from the group and looked out a window. The kid's attitude troubled Juel, but he said to himself, "I've just got to forget him and focus on the ones who are paying attention."

That particular Sunday, Juel was teaching the story of Jesus' baptism in Mark, and he said to the junior highs, "Mark says that when Jesus was baptized, the heavens were ripped apart. Do you know that when Mark says 'ripped apart' he uses a variation of the Greek word *schizo*, like our word 'schizophrenic'? What Mark is saying is that there is this curtain hanging between heaven and earth and that when Jesus was baptized, *schizo*, it was ripped open and you could see into heaven. Do you know what that means, kids? That means we can see God because of the baptism of Jesus, we can actually get to God."

The kid on the end, the kid who did not want to be there, squirmed in his seat. He turned and said, "That isn't what it means."

Juel, a little irritated, looked at him and said, "Oh, yeah, what does it mean?"

"It doesn't mean that we can get to God," the kid said. "It means that God can get to us. And the world isn't safe any-more." Juel knew immediately that the kid had gotten it right. It isn't that we can get to God but that God can get to us.

Paul would agree. "Of this gospel, I was made a minister," he says. Paul didn't get to God. God got to Paul. That is the way it is with ministry and ministers. Something outside of us, the mystery of God, summons us into a place we would not have chosen on our own—into a role we would never have dreamed for ourselves. Of this gospel, I *was made* a minister.

Ministers may appear to be peculiar in this regard. In our culture, it seems strange to do anything at the summons of a force outside ourselves. Our culture tends to say we ought to follow our inner dreams, live out our true selves, that sort of thing. It would seem odd for an architect or a television anchor or an artist to say, "I didn't choose this; I was chosen for it. I was made an architect." But the truth is that what is true about ministry is true of all human beings at their best and deepest. Finally what it means to be human is to be called to something beyond our own little dreams and goals, to be fashioned into bearers of the mystery of God that stands at the center of life.

When I was a little boy and did something I should not have done, my mother would sometimes say to me, "Now son, that was uncalled for!" That is an interesting phrase, isn't it? *"Uncalled for."* As if goodness were something that has to be *called for.* As if being a human being in the best sense is to be someone who is called for. It may sound strange, this talk of being "called for," but the older I get the more I realize that one of the deepest fears of any human being is that, at the end of the day, we will not be called for. We are terrified that we could live our lives setting the clock, minding the store, tapping the keyboard, making the payments on the Lexus and the boat, but finally not be called for. How sad to come to the end of our days knowing that no mystery outside ourselves summoned us to a life of adventure and depth and costly risk and powerful meaning, a life that we would not have chosen

41

on our own, a life we had to be summoned to take up. What is true of ministers is true of all human beings. "Of this gospel, I *was made* a minister."

Many years ago, my family and I worshiped at a church located near the campus of a major university. This church prides itself on having many university and seminary professors in the congregation. It is a very learned and intellectually alert congregation. One Wednesday night, I was at a family night supper and found myself seated next to a man I did not know. We struck up a conversation, and he said, "I haven't seen you before around the church. Have you been in the church long?"

"No," I said, "we just moved to town. How about you? How long have you been involved in this church?"

"Oh my Lord," he replied. "I've been a part of this church all my life. In fact, I'm the last nonintellectual left in this congregation."

"You're kidding."

"No, I'm not," he said. "I have not understood a sermon that has been preached here in twenty-five years."

He went on to tell me, though, that he would never leave this church. He said that every Monday night he and three or four others from the congregation take the church van and go to a nearby youth correctional institute. "We go up there and we play table tennis with the inmates. We do Bible study with them. Mainly we just get to know them and try to show them that we care." And then he added, "I started doing this because I thought it's the kind of thing that a Christian ought to do. But now, I would not miss a Monday night because I have found that it nourishes my soul." Then he paused and said, "You know, you can't prove any of the promises of God in advance. But I found that if you live them, they're true. Every one."

I think that what he said may be the best sermon preached in that church in twenty-five years. What he said is the word of a person who has been summoned from outside himself or herself. He started this work because of an inner ought, but found that he was actually in the presence of the God who calls. "Of this gospel, I was made a minister."

Be warned, the God who calls to all of us will take us places we never dreamed we would go, take us on an adventure we never imaged, provoke us to say things we never thought we would say and to do things we never envisioned we would do.

They buried Grace Thomas in a cemetery near the First Baptist Church of Decatur, Georgia. Grace Thomas was the daughter of a streetcar conductor in Birmingham, Alabama. She fell in love with a boy from Atlanta, a Georgia Tech student. She moved to Atlanta. She married him, and, in order to support the family, she started working as a secretary at the state capitol. She got kind of interested in politics and law. So she decided that she was going to go to law school at night. Grace Thomas, full-time secretary, full-time wife and mother, and then full-time law student.

When she finished law school, her family wondered what she would do. Would she keep on at the capitol? Would she start a private practice? She thought about it and then she startled her family by saying that she was going to run for the office of governor of Georgia.

In 1954, Grace Thomas ran for governor. There were nine candidates—eight men and Grace—but there was really only one issue; it was 1954 and the Supreme Court decision in the case known as *Brown v. the Board of Education* had led to integrating the public schools. Eight of the candidates said this was an outrage and the citizens of Georgia ought to resist it with every ounce of strength. But one candidate, Grace, said, "It looks like justice to me. We ought to rejoice."

Her campaign slogan was "Say Grace at the polls." Not many people did. She ran last, and her family was relieved that she had gotten politics out of her system. But she hadn't. And in 1962, she decided to run again for governor. She ran last again, and this time the political environment was intensely hostile. The Civil Rights Movement was taking hold, and Grace's progressive position on race was clear. There were threats on her life, and members of her family began to travel with her for protection.

One day, she took her campaign to the little town of Louisville, Georgia. At the center of Louisville is not a court-house or a war monument but an old slave market, a place where human beings were bought and sold. When Grace surveyed the town, she decided she would deliver her speech on the porch of the slave market. She stood under the canopy and addressed the merchants and farmers who had gathered to hear her. What she told them was that the old had passed away and the new had come. "It is time," she said, "for Georgians black and white to join hands and work together for communities of harmony and peace."

Suddenly the speech was interrupted by a man who shouted angrily, "Are you a Communist?"

"No," she said, "I'm not."

"Well then where did you get those dern ideas?"

Grace Thomas thought for a moment, and then she pointed to the steeple of a nearby church. "I got them over there," she said, "in Sunday school."

Grace Thomas was in a place she never dreamed she would be, bearing witness to the gospel of reconciliation, saying things she probably never imagined she would say and standing for a love wider than all human imagining. If some-one had said to her, "How in the world did you ever choose *this?*" she would almost certainly have answered, "*Choose* it? I didn't choose this. I was chosen for it." She would surely have known what Paul meant when he wrote, "By the grace of God, of this gospel I was made a minister."

# Here I Am, Send Me

## Jeremiah A. Wright, Jr.

In the year that King Uzziah died, I saw the Lord sitting on a throne, high and lofty; and the hem of his robe filled the temple. Seraphs were in attendance above him; each had six wings: with two they covered their faces, and with two they covered their feet, and with two they flew. And one called to another and said:
"Holy, holy, holy is the LORD of hosts;
the whole earth is full of his glory."
The pivots on the thresholds shook at the voices of those who called, and the house filled with smoke. And I said: "Woe is me! I am lost, for I am a man of unclean lips, and I live among a people of unclean lips; yet my eyes have seen the King, the LORD of hosts!"
Then one of the seraphs flew to me, holding a live coal that had been taken from the altar with a pair of tongs. The seraph touched my mouth with it and said: "Now that this has touched your lips, your guilt has departed and your sin is blotted out." Then I heard the voice of the Lord saying, "Whom shall I send, and who will go for us?" And I said, "Here am I; send me!"

—Isaiah 6:1-8

The theme, "Here am I; send me!" taken from Isaiah 6, is fascinating to me because we often skip over the third word in that theme, Here am *I*. I guess I should start by underlining what I mean by that "I." I don't know if you've ever heard of Charles G. Adams or not. In preaching circles in America, Dr. Adams is known as the "Harvard Hooper." Charlie is a graduate of Harvard University. With his M.Div. from Harvard, and his being the pastor of the Hartsfield Memorial Baptist Church in Detroit, Michigan, for thirty years now, he is a mentor of mine and someone I have admired for many, many years.

He is the grandnephew of Gordon Hancock, the man whose church was closest to the campus when I was in college. We used to walk up there to church on Sundays, those of us who did not have automobiles, and that was most of us back in the fifties. And that's where I met Charlie. Charlie is a world-renowned preacher, and in 1975 I asked a friend of mine, Bishop McKinley Young, if he could get Charles to come to our church.

Our church at that time had about a hundred, or a hundred and fifteen members, and I didn't know if we could afford Charlie and I knew that he preached for Bishop McKinley. And McKinley told me, "I'm not going to call him, you call him." So I called him, and he came and has been coming to our church every year since 1975. And he would always invite me to come preach at his church. Now if you could hear Charles Adams preach, you would understand why every year I had an excuse as to why I couldn't go.

He would ask me in October, "Well, could you come next April?" And I would say, "I've got a funeral that weekend." And I always made an excuse for not going, and I kept dodging and ducking and dodging and ducking, until in October of 1979 when he stood up to preach at our church, he announced in his opening remarks that he wanted our choir to come sing for his tenth anniversary the next April.

And everybody broke out applauding. He said, "I want you to give a concert in the afternoon. I also want you to sing that morning because your pastor is going to preach my tenth anniversary service." And they all started applauding again, and I said, "Oh, God." And I really had butterflies. I did not feel good about it; it was a traumatic experience for me.

My dad pastored in Philadelphia for forty-two years, and every Saturday night of my early years of ministry he and I would talk on the phone, and he would always ask me this question. You know how you have a car that's gassed up? He would ask me, "Are you ghost up?" Meaning, do I have the Holy Ghost? Are you ready for tomorrow morning? On that Saturday night before preaching at Hartford Memorial, I called him from Detroit, from the hotel, right before I preached at Charles Adams's church and he said, "Are you in Detroit this week?" And I said, "Yes, sir."

And he said, "Are you ghost up?" I said, "No." He said, "What?" I said, "No I am not." He said, "What do you mean, no you're not? It's midnight on a Saturday!" I said, "I know what time it is." He said, "What's wrong?" I said, "Daddy, I can't preach at Charles Adams's church." He said, "Why?"

I said, "I can't preach like Charles Adams." He said, "God didn't call you to preach like Charles Adams. God called you to preach like Jeremiah Wright. Those folk know who their pastor is. They know how he preaches. You preach Jeremiah Wright's sermon and go on back home!"

Well, that piece of advice that he gave me stuck with me, because what I've found out in ministry is that so many times all of us have mentors and models in ministry: Bishop Vashti Mackenzie or Ann Lightner-Fuller or Prathia Hall Wynn or Charles Adams or Fred Samson or George Buttrick. And we try to be like them. But God didn't call you to be like them, God called you to be *you*. So you don't say, "Here am I— Charles Adams's clone. Here am I, Ken Whalum's clone." No, you say, "Here am *I*."

Who are *you*? What unique experiences has God led you through? In the book of Jeremiah, God says to Jeremiah, "I called *you* in your mother's womb." I'm talking about *you*. I'm not talking about Isaiah or Ezekiel or Daniel. God was saying I know *you*. I knit you together. I understand who you are and I want you to use the gifts that I've given you and the experiences that I've shown you. I want you to be *you* in terms of preaching the gospel, in terms of spreading love abroad in the hearts of those to whom you are sent to serve. That's the "I" that you offer to God.

# On This Rock

## Barbara Brown Taylor

*Now when Jesus came into the district of Caesarea Philippi, he asked his disciples, "Who do people say that the Son of Man is?" And they said, "Some say John the Baptist, but others Elijah, and still others Jeremiah or one of the prophets." He said to them, "But who do you say that I am?" Simon Peter answered, "You are the Messiah, the Son of the living God." And Jesus answered him, "Blessed are you, Simon son of Jonah! For flesh and blood has not revealed this to you, but my Father in heaven. And I tell you, you are Peter, and on this rock I will build my church, and the gates of Hades will not prevail against it. I will give you the keys of the kingdom of heaven, and whatever you bind on earth will be bound in heaven, and whatever you loose on earth will be loosed in heaven." Then he sternly ordered the disciples not to tell anyone that he was the Messiah.*

*From that time on, Jesus began to show his disciples that he must go to Jerusalem and undergo great suffering at the hands of the elders and chief priests and scribes, and be killed, and on the third day be raised. And Peter took him aside and began to rebuke him, saying, "God forbid it, Lord! This must never happen to you." But he turned and said to Peter, "Get behind me, Satan! You are a stumbling block to me; for you are setting your mind not on divine things but on human things."*

—Matthew 16:13-23

A couple of years ago, when Jim Waits first started to revive the Fund for Theological Education, he told me what kind of people he was looking for—the brightest and best possible candidates for ministry—people with brains, heart, faith, and character, who might be persuaded to work long hours for low pay if they had any idea how vital their vocations might turn out to be. So you are the ones. I wondered who you would turn out to be.

He was looking for people who might save the church, although he would never have put it that way. Only God can save the church, and yet God has, from the beginning, chosen to do that by choosing certain people and asking them to lead. Sometimes the asking is spectacular—burning bushes, descending doves, that kind of thing—but far more often it is as ordinary as someone saying, "Have you ever thought about becoming a minister? I think you'd be good at that." Sometimes it even comes through the mail, in the form of a letter from some outfit down in Atlanta that wants to give you money to study theology.

You are the ones. Whatever you decide to do about it, you have been invited to consider vocations in the church, and already you are getting a taste of the high expectations. How are your grades? Your prayer life? Are you managing to keep up with your service to others as well as your studies? Have people begun to apologize to you if they say a curse word in your presence? In this vocation, the currency is not technical skill or billable hours. In this vocation, the currency is the quality of your life. It is how much people see Christ when they look at you.

This is so because the church survives by sacraments—by outward and visible signs of inward and spiritual graces—not only water, bread, and wine, but also men and women who are willing to live in a certain way. Creatures of flesh, we learn best by flesh. Our bodies are primary sources of revelation for us. God knows that if nothing else works to get our attention, then what happens in our bodies will often do the trick. Cool water on a hot day, the weight of a sleeping child in your arms, food shared with strangers, a pounding heart in the middle of the night—these are the things that make theologians out of us. Our struggle to make meaning out of them is what fuels our search for God, and that is why the church needs sacraments. We contemplate all that we cannot see by contemplating what we can.

Some churches count two sacraments and some count seven, but the number is not as important as the pattern. Once we have learned to recognize God's presence in holy communion, then we are better equipped to recognize God's presence wherever bread is taken, blessed, broken, and given. Once we have learned to recognize God's gift of new life in holy baptism, then we are better equipped to recognize that gift wherever water flows to cleanse and refresh.

Last week I took part in a celebration of holy communion with people from many different faith traditions. When it came time to pass the bread around the circle, I watched Baptists feed Presbyterians who fed Episcopalians who fed Methodists. When the bread came to the one Quaker in the group, he smiled at the woman holding the loaf, put his hand on her shoulder, and stepped back so that she could feed the next person in the circle. He put his hand on that person's shoulder too, so that the circle was unbroken even though he did not eat the bread.

Watching him, I remembered what another Quaker taught me years ago.

"How do you survive without sacraments?" I asked him.

"Oh, we have a sacrament," he said, "a very powerful one. It is the sacrament of another human being. When we look into one another's faces, that is our bread and our wine, our constant reminder that God is with us."

It is a sacrament all Christians share, whether we count it or not. Over and over again, when human beings have asked the invisible God to come out of hiding, God has said, "You're not up to it, I promise, but I will give you a reasonable facsimile. Here is a neighbor; someone just like you. Treat her as you would treat me. Give him whatever you want to give me, and trust that I have received the gift."

For better or worse, clergy provide congregations with lots of opportunities to practice this sacrament of another human being in a particularly focused way. If someone is furious with God, then clergy make great punching bags. If someone is grateful to God, then clergy may come to work and find homemade pound cakes or jelly jars full of wild-flowers sitting in front of their doors. Both kinds of gestures go with the territory, since churches survive by sacraments and clergy tend to be identified as the most sacramental people around.

If you decide to go ahead and do this, then your parish-ioners are going to watch *everything* you do—not only the way you run a meeting or hold a baby, but also how fast you drive your car and whether you bite your fingernails. They will do this because you are their parson—their representa-tive person—who stands on the tipsy edge between God and God's people, having promised to be true to them both. People will watch you to see what a life of faith really looks like. They will watch you because they want to see Jesus, or at least one of Jesus' best friends.

Living this sacramental life turns out to be quite a job description, and depending on your personality it can make you or break you. I belong to a large circle of friends who occasionally suffer from what psychologists call "impos-tor's syndrome." Maybe you will recognize the symptoms yourself. It comes on you when you are in some gathering of people who start telling you how wonderful you are— how full of promise you are, what an inspiration you are, how they hope all of their children will grow up to be just like you.

No matter how hard you have worked to earn accolades like that, you start feeling a little damp under your arms. Little bees start buzzing around inside your head and whatever modest, accommodating thing you happen to be saying back to the person in front of you, there is a cartoon balloon over your head with what you are really thinking inside of it: "I have somehow gotten in here by mistake, and I need to get out of here as soon as I can before someone discovers who I really am and asks me to leave." Does that sound familiar? Then you too may have impostor's syndrome. High achievers are especially susceptible. Ministerial candidates are doomed.

That is why I asked Simon Peter to be with us here tonight—Simon, son of Jonah, nicknamed Rocky, who in ten short verses of Matthew's Gospel goes from cornerstone of the church to satanic stumbling block, and all for the love of Jesus. The story of his rise and fall is a lot longer in Matthew than it is in Mark or Luke, and it is not about recognizing who Jesus really is, either. As far as Matthew is concerned, that happened a couple of chapters earlier, when Jesus stilled the storm, saved Peter from drowning, and everyone in the boat worshiped him, saying, "Truly you are the Son of God."

While Peter reaffirms that recognition at Caesarea Philippi, Jesus' identity has already been established. He is the Son of God, and his disciples know it. What has not yet been established is the identity of the church. Once Jesus has used up his body and ascended into heaven, what sacramental presence will remain on earth? What kind of body will the church be, and what kind of virtues will its leaders embody?

There were at least twelve people present when Jesus began to investigate the answers to these questions. "Who do people say that the Son of Man is?" he asked them. Were the disciples listening to people? Did they know how to read people's hungers by the foods they named? "Some say John the Baptist, but others Elijah, and still others Jeremiah or one of the prophets," the disciples replied. Those are all names pronounced by people who are ravenous for change. Good, Jesus said, so you heard them. The church needs to know how to listen to people.

"But who do you say that I am?" he asked them next. Do you also know how to listen to God? Not to your own experience, although that is important. Not to your own reason, although that is important too—but to the still, small voice of God inside you. Do you know how to recognize that voice?

"You are the Messiah, the Son of the living God," Peter blurted out, and Jesus blessed him on the spot. Jesus made Peter the subject of his own little beatitude, but like all of the other beatitudes this one had a surprise ending. "Blessed are you, Simon son of Jonah!" *Lucky Rocky!* "For flesh and blood has not revealed this to you, but my Father in heaven." *For you did not come up with this answer on your own.* So good again, Peter. You heard God. The church needs to know how to listen to God.

According to Matthew, that was enough to convince Jesus that Peter could be trusted with the keys to the kingdom. If Peter knew how to listen to all the voices in and around him—and if he could still tell which one was the voice of God—then he would not get far lost for long. People could say whatever they said around him, whether that was good, bad, or ugly. He would listen, but he would not get bowled over. As rock of the church, Peter's chief virtue was that he knew the sound of God.

And then the next moment he forgot it. The moment Jesus started talking about the certainty of his own suffering and death, Peter clamped his hands over his ears. "God forbid it, Lord!" he rebuked Jesus (he *rebuked* Jesus!), "This must never happen to you!" And just like that, Peter the Rock became Satan-the-stumbling-block, because he got his own voice confused with the voice of God.

It was just a little slip. Please note that Jesus did not take the keys away from Peter, or change his name to "Pebble." Peter remained in the inner circle along with James and John—one of the three people who Jesus wanted with him when things got especially intense. Peter was only Satan for a second, when he forgot the sound of God. Then he remembered it again. Then he forgot it again. Then he remembered it again, and who knows how many times the cycle repeated itself after Matthew blew out the candle and closed his book.

On one hand, Jesus' choice of Peter seems almost ironic—a kind of sad parable about the true identity of the church—remembering, forgetting, remembering, forgetting.

"Though all become deserters because of you, I will never desert you," Peter said at the last supper table, but before the night was over he had forgotten three times. "Jesus of Nazareth? I do not know the man."

On the other hand, Jesus' choice of Peter seems a gesture of pure compassion. We are all far more like Peter than we are like Jesus, after all. If Peter is our model, then no one ever has to suffer from impostor's syndrome. God knows who we are. God has known us all along, and is still willing to trust us with the church—not because we are capable of drumming up much excellence on our own but because we are willing to keep remembering what we keep forgetting, and to keep listening for that voice that rings above the rest. Like Peter, our chief virtue is that we know the sound of God.

When I was an FTE fellow contemplating ordination twenty-five years ago, I found a wise and moody priest whose name could have been Peter. The poor man was crawling with seminarians. We were all over him like bees on honey, because he seemed to have the right word for each one of us. Sometimes we pestered him so badly that he had to slam doors in our faces and tell us to *go away*. The first time he yelled at me I thought I would slide to the floor and die right there. Then he took me into his kitchen and fed me leftover Chinese.

I adored him, which was hard on him, I know. One day I told him that my biggest fear about ordination was the perfection thing—impersonating Jesus in front of a whole lot of people who would see right through me—and he said, "Oh lovey, that's not your job. If you decide to do this, then you're not promising to be perfect. You're just consenting to be visible—to let other people watch you while you try to figure out what real life is all about." Remembering, forgetting, remembering, forgetting.

What rock could be a better sacrament than a flawed and sometimes faithless rock? Who could leave more room for God to be God? And what better outward and visible sign of God's inward and spiritual grace could there be than a man or a woman who gets it right and then gets it wrong but keeps on trying to *get it*—visibly, in front of a whole lot of people who are trying to do the same thing?

So you are the ones—the brightest and best possible candidates for ministry—the ones with brains, heart, faith, and character enough to shore up a sagging church? Well, are you? If you are, then do I have good news for you! You are not Jesus. That position has already been filled. Instead, you are Peter's children—sons and daughters of the rock on whom Christ has built the church, so that even the gates of Hades will not prevail against it. Is that easier for you to say yes to? If it is, then you inherit a share in Peter's beatitude too: blessed are you, for you did not come up with that answer on your own.

Glory to God whose power, working in us, can do infinitely more than we can ask or imagine. Glory to God from generation to generation in the church, and in Christ Jesus forever and ever. Amen.

# Two Places at the Same Time

## Brad R. Braxton

> *I, John, your brother who share with you in Jesus the persecution and the kingdom and the patient endurance, was on the island called Patmos because of the word of God and the testimony of Jesus. I was in the spirit on the Lord's day, and I heard behind me a loud voice like a trumpet saying, "Write in a book what you see and send it to the seven churches, to Ephesus, to Smyrna, to Pergamum, to Thyatira, to Sardis, to Philadelphia, and to Laodicea."*
>
> —Revelation 1:9-11

"Here" and "there" are adverbs suggesting alternative locations. Something that is here is in our immediate environs, and in order to retrieve something there, we have to leave here and go there. Then there becomes here, and here becomes there. Spatially, here and there are mutually exclusive, because you can't be in two places at the same time.

Wouldn't it be awesome if we could be in two places at the same time? If we could suspend the laws of physics and collapse the restricting space between here and there, our lives would be much more interesting. If you could be in two places at the same time, you could be in class on a Monday morning at nine, while snoozing in the bed. If you could be in two places at the same time, you could simultaneously visit two sets of relatives in different parts of the country and spend an equal amount of time with each.

If you could be in two places at the same time, you could watch the brilliant sun rise in the east as it paints its orange rays on the canvas of the morning, while simultaneously beholding the heavenly jeweler place diamond star studs on the ebony cloth of the western horizon. If you could be in two places at the same time, you could shop till you drop in Parisian boutiques, while shaking your pants while you dance to the calypso beat of a Jamaican steel band in Montego Bay. Wouldn't it be nice to be in two places at the same time?

Who knows? With the breakthroughs of genetic cloning, maybe fifty years from now it might be physically possible for someone possessing your exact DNA to be there while you are here. But until such genetic engineering is perfected, in the natural realm it is impossible for people to be in two places at the same time. I am well aware of our limitations in the natural realm. But I wonder: do these limitations hold in the supernatural realm of the spirit—in the realm where God resides?

In the natural world, I have no formula yet for how you can be in two places at the same time. When the semester begins, you will have to get up every morning and go to class. I wish I knew the secret, but I don't; so keep your alarm clocks in working condition. In order to be in two places at the same time in the natural realm, you will have to consult my colleagues in the physics and biology departments at the university.

However, I have stumbled across some insights about how to be in two places at the same time in the spiritual realm. I ran across this life-changing secret not searching scholarly journals, or listening to talk radio. This breakthrough came from reading the Scriptures. I was perusing the first chapter of the book of Revelation, and it dawned on me with a fresh force that we can be in two places at the same time.

In Revelation 1, there is a Christian brother named John who tells us that he was suffering persecution patiently for his belief in Christ. John also tells us the locale of his suffering: "I, John,... was on the island called Patmos."

Patmos—one of the islands in the Aegean Sea about thirty-seven miles southwest of Miletus. Patmos—a place where, according to the Roman historian Tacitus, political offenders of the Roman Empire were imprisoned. Patmos—the Alcatraz of the first-century world. Boat tickets to Patmos were normally one-way. Offenders went in, but they did not come out. If you were on Patmos, you had offended the emperor in one way or another. John, a Christian brother, was on Patmos all by himself. Or was he by himself?

As quiet as it's kept, maybe there is somebody else on Patmos along with John. Pastoral ministry has taught me that Patmos is not just a place; Patmos is also an experience.

Patmos—that's when you have more months than you have money. Patmos—that's when a cherished relationship has been tarnished by a corrosive deception. Patmos—that's where vicious opposition to your ministry arises from people you thought supported you. Patmos—that's the place in your life where you do what's right—in school, on the job, in the family, and in the church—but Satan is still wearing you out. As quiet as it's kept and behind the veneers of your smiles, somebody here, regardless of age and station, is on Patmos with John.

Because of his testimony about Jesus, John was banished, but in Revelation 1:10, John also declares, "I was in the spirit on the Lord's day." He just told us he was on Patmos—that's one place. Then he says that he was also in the spirit on the Lord's day—that's another place.

He was on Patmos, but simultaneously in the spirit. He was living on a prison island, but still residing in the Holy Ghost. He was surrounded on all sides by the briny deep of the Aegean Sea, but still able to get in the flow of God's spirit. John had made a supernatural breakthrough. You *can* be in two places at the same time. John was in a jam, but he didn't allow his jam to block him from getting to Jesus.

There are some Christians, and even some ministers, who go to pieces as soon as trouble arises. Some believers only have testimonies when blue skies smile at them and when bluebirds serenade them. These Christians lose their testimonies when the sky darkens and the winds of opposition start whirling, as surely they will in ministry. In Revelation 1, John said, in effect: "I'm not going to lose my testimony. I'm not copping out on God. I'm not going to wallow in self-pity, nor am I going to throw in the towel. The emperor gave me a one-way ticket to Patmos. But what Caesar does not know is that I can be in two places at the same time. Patmos is my physical mailing address, but my real location—the place where I truly live, the point of my ultimate orientation—is the spirit of God. I was on Patmos, but I was also in the spirit on the Lord's day."

Anybody aspiring to Christian leadership needs to learn, like John, how to be in two places at the same time. Even if trouble, difficulty, or disappointment is your mailing address, if you also reside in the spirit, you'll still be able to sing, "The Lord will make a way...somehow!" Maybe your Patmos is doubt from your family and ridicule from your friends because they just can't understand this call to ministry that you are feeling. But if you are also in the spirit, you can still press on declaring, "Ain't gonna let nobody turn me 'round!"

Maybe your Patmos is a recent trip to a cemetery, having laid to rest a loved one. But if you are also in the spirit, you can still say with thanksgiving, "The Lord giveth, and the Lord taketh away. Blessed be the name of the Lord." Those who are interested in keeping their sanity in an insane world need to learn how to be in two places at the same time. John said, "I was on Patmos, but I was also in the spirit on the Lord's day."

First, if we want to be in two places at the same time, we, as God's people, need to define ourselves not by *where* we are, but by *whose* we are. We need to define ourselves, especially in ministry, not by *what* we possess, but by *who* possesses us.

John said it was "the Lord's day." Now upon first glance, this phrase, "the Lord's day" seems rather straightforward. But this little phrase, "the Lord's day," is like a crate of dynamite meant to explode the arrogance of Roman imperial culture.

John is writing in the late first century. And for more than a century, the Roman Empire has ruled the Mediterranean world with a fierce military machine. In the late first century, a political and religious phenomenon—the Imperial Cult—was beginning to develop. Persons in the Roman Empire were encouraged, as part of their religious observance, to offer religious rites in honor of the emperor. Occasionally, some imperial devotees went so far as to elevate the emperor to divine status.

Anybody with half a brain knew that Caesar was in control. Caesar was running the show. It was Caesar's world; it was Caesar's day.

If anybody should have known how powerful Caesar was, it should have been John, because John more than likely had been banished to Patmos because of his refusal to give honor to Caesar. Everybody knew that Caesar was Lord. Everybody, that is, except John.

John insists: "I was in the spirit on the *Lord's day*. Caesar is not Lord. Jesus is Lord! I know who really has control. Caesar might have Rome in his hand, but the whole world is in the Lord's hands. I belong to God. You belong to God. Time belongs to God. Even Caesar belongs to God. It's not Caesar's day. It's the *Lord's day*! Thus, I will define myself, not by *where* I am, but by *whose* I am."

John offers us a compelling example of the pastoral imagination. He demonstrates that life and ministry are never exhausted by what happens on the material, visible level. There is another realm of existence that allows us to be faithful witnesses, even when we are under fire.

For a ministry that matters, we need to know how to be in the Spirit even when we're on Patmos. For a ministry that matters, define yourself not by *where* you are, but by *whose* you are. Define yourself not by *what* you possess, but by *who* possesses you.

Second, if we want to be in two places at the same time, we must never allow our problems to rob us of our praise. Theological education and ministry may be anemic in some locations because we have lost the praise of God in our pursuit of academic and ministerial excellence.

When one reads the book of Revelation, one enters a world of exuberant praise. The book of Revelation is not a calendar of cataclysmic events to be read literally. Revelation is majestic poetry exhorting us to live worshipful lives here as a dress rehearsal for the ceaseless, exuberant worship that occurs in the heavenly realm.

Praise of God is at the center of this book. Praise should be the posture of people who realize that Patmos is never ultimate. We praise God because there is another realm where "the Beast" has been conquered and where the devil is unemployed. When we learn how to live in the power of God's spirit in spite of our circumstances, we board an express train to victory, because our problems will not prohibit our praise.

One sign of spiritual and theological maturity is when we can look at our problems and say, "Hallelujah, anyhow." I don't know where the fall tuition is coming from, but, "Hallelujah, anyhow." I have some devilish deacons and some tricky trustees I'm dealing with at the church, but, "Hallelujah, anyhow." My parents don't understand, my spouse doesn't understand, I don't even understand this call on my life, but, "Hallelujah, anyhow."

God has revealed to me an intriguing spiritual truth. I did not learn this truth in graduate school. I discovered this while matriculating in the school of hard knocks as a pastor. The pathway to power is to learn how to praise God in the midst of our problems and pain.

In Psalm 22:3, the writer declares that God inhabits, or is enthroned on, the praise of God's people. Praise is God's dwelling place. Where praise is, God is. When we praise God, even though we are on Patmos, we erect a sanctuary above our heads, and God's spirit comes in and fills the place.

You might have a problem on Patmos, but in your sanctuary above, you can still have a revival service. As long as you are down in the mouth and down in spirit, the demonic has robbed you of your ability to be in two places at the same time. But when you praise God, even in the midst of your problems, you construct a tabernacle over your problems.

Praise creates a sacred space over your problems, and in that space you can find the rest and the resources you need to withstand the storm. You might be on Patmos. Yet when you learn how to praise God in the midst of your Patmos, you create an alternative spiritual reality.

African American slaves understood well the spiritual phenomenon of being in two places at the same time. They knew there was power in praise. Praise is the passionate attestation of God's sovereignty. Praise is an essential building block of the pastoral imagination.

My African American ancestors praised God in the morning. They praised God in the heat of the day. They praised God in the brush arbor at midnight. They assembled in praise circles and danced, shouted, and praised the true and living God. In spite of the indignities and atrocities of slavery, they were never inhibited in their praise.

For many of my ancestors, Patmos was the plantation. Yet through their praise and prayers they also lived in the spirit. As my ancestors said, they sent up "timber" every day through their prayers and praise, building another location in which their spirits could live. Their unswerving dependence on God's spirit was not psychological escapism, but rather a marvelous example of theological imagination.

They never ever retreated from life in the physical world, with its joys and sorrows. But at the same time, they constructed an alternative world where their spirits could find respite, if only for a moment. That's what I call pastoral imagination. That's why my ancestors would sing triumphantly:

Over my head, I hear music in the air.
Over my head, I see glory in the air.
There must be, there's got to be—I am persuaded there is a
    God, somewhere.

They learned how to be in two places at the same time. They had chains on their bodies, but still they were free in the spirit.

I don't know what your Patmos is, but for a ministry that matters, learn how to be in two places at the same time. If it's dark on Patmos, there is light in the spirit. If it's lonely on Patmos, there is fellowship in the spirit. If there is sadness on Patmos, there is joy—unspeakable joy—in the spirit.

If there is a dead end on Patmos, there is a "way out of no way" in the spirit. If there is sickness on Patmos, there is healing in the spirit. If you have anxiety about your ministry on Patmos, there is a peace that passes all understanding in the spirit. If it's Good Friday on Patmos, it is resurrection morning in the spirit.

I refuse to be defined by my Patmos. Through God's spirit, I am able to be in two places at the same time. Amen.

# The Chance for a Sub-version

## Walter Brueggemann

*Bring forth the people who are blind, yet have eyes,*
   *who are deaf, yet have ears!*
*Let all the nations gather together,*
   *and let the peoples assemble.*
*Who among them declared this,*
   *and foretold to us the former things?*
*Let them bring their witnesses to justify them,*
   *and let them hear and say, "It is true."*
*You are my witnesses, says the* Lord,
   *and my servant whom I have chosen,*
*so that you may know and believe me*
   *and understand that I am he.*
*Before me no god was formed,*
   *nor shall there be any after me.*
*I, I am the* Lord,
   *and besides me there is no savior.*
*I declared and saved and proclaimed,*
   *when there was no strange god among you;*
   *and you are my witnesses, says the* Lord.
*I am God, and also henceforth I am He;*
   *there is no one who can deliver from my hand;*
   *I work and who can hinder it?*
                              —Isaiah 43:8-13

*"When you hear of wars and insurrections, do not be ter-*
*rified; for these things must take place first, but the end*
*will not follow immediately." Then he said to them,*
*"Nation will rise against nation, and kingdom against*
*kingdom; there will be great earthquakes, and in various*
*places famines and plagues; and there will be dreadful*
*portents and great signs from heaven.*

*"But before all this occurs, they will arrest you and*
*persecute you; they will hand you over to synagogues and*
*prisons, and you will be brought before kings and gover-*
*nors because of my name. This will give you an opportu-*
*nity to testify. So make up your minds not to prepare your*
*defense in advance; for I will give you words and a wis-*
*dom that none of your opponents will be able to withstand*
*or contradict. You will be betrayed even by parents and*
*brothers, by relatives and friends; and they will put some*
*of you to death. You will be hated by all because of my*
*name. But not a hair of your head will perish. By your*
*endurance you will gain your souls."*

—Luke 21:9-19

I am delighted to have this chance to think with you about
these important questions of vocation. You may have
noticed that both of these texts from Isaiah and Luke talk
about bearing witness and testifying. I thought that the theme
of the mission of the church and ministerial vocations is an
important one for us to think about together. We are concerned about witnesses and testimony when truth is contested and when it becomes necessary to go to court. When
there is enough agreement on the truth on a matter to settle
out of court, no witnesses are called, no depositions are taken,
and no testimony is offered. There was a long time in the
United States when the claims of Christian faith were easily
accommodated to U.S. culture and there was no particular
dispute about the truth. The church mostly did not think
about the dangerous task of testimony. You may know the

Greek word for *witness* is "martyr." We didn't talk much about being "martyrs." The notion of testimony as a risky enterprise seemed like an ancient, old-fashioned idea that no longer pertained to modern society.

But now we live in a society where truth is again contested even among us; there is need for adjudication of the truth that arises in part because people are so bewildered about the new strange world in which God has put us. The truth is contested among us because we have strongly invested advocacies that butt against each other forcefully and they cannot be reconciled. In such an environment, dispute is an inescapable fact and therefore we need witnesses.

That is the way it was in the ancient world of the Jews in Isaiah 43. This remarkable poet imagines, in a poetic idiom, that there will be a trial to settle these disputed claims. On the one hand, there are the dominant claims of the Babylonian Empire legitimated by the great gods of the empire who seem so powerful and absolute. On the other side, against that imperial version of reality, this poet summoned exiled Jews to give an alternative version of reality, what I have called a "sub-version," that centers in the claims of the God of Israel who creates and saves. This text says to these Jews in exile, "You're my witnesses and this is what you shall say: 'Before me there was no God. There's none after me. I am the Lord God and besides me there's no savior.'" "You say that," God says to the Jews. There is no other savior even among the gods of the empire!

It was not different in the early church. The early church spent a great deal of time contesting the claims of dominant culture. In that dominant culture, the early church offered a sub-version of reality that claimed that the suffering, death, and resurrection of Jesus was the defining clue to reality. In Jesus, the church has seen that all dominant versions of reality are fraudulent. So Luke writes, "But before all this occurs, they will arrest you and persecute you; and they will hand you over...and you will be brought before kings and governors because of my name.... This will give you an opportunity to testify." The two situations of exilic Jews and early Christians are paralleled; the matter is contested and Jews, and then Christians, claim a sub-version of reality that subverts all dominant notions of reality.

I believe that the mission of the church in our culture and Christian ministry is now in such a context. Of course it is possible to do Christian ministry that accommodates and becomes chaplain of the status quo, but not for people like us. I imagine that in the days to come the crucial issue of our lives is the extent to which we sign on to the dominant versions of reality and the ways in which we embrace this sub-version of reality as the defining truth of our life and the central perspective on our future.

The sub-version among Jews in the book of Isaiah turns out to be a vision of justice for which the world waits, suffering love that will break the cycles of brutality. The sub-version in the early church makes the claim that Friday suffering breaks the denial of the world, and Sunday victory overwhelms the despair of the world. For sure, the narcotics of denial and despair are overcome in the story of Jesus.

I think that is how it is now among us. This sub-version of faith has nothing to do with being liberal rather than conservative or being conservative rather than liberal. It has to do with this question, whether the dominant force of technological, electronic, military consumerism is to have the final say in the world, whether the practices of greed, amnesia, despair, alienation, and a dozen other pathologies are to shape the world for the sake of the privileged, or whether the covenantal dreams of Moses and the deep hopes of Jeremiah and the transformative love of Jesus will draw us to an alternative notion of the world.

In the hands of the poets, this either/or of contested faith is stated clearly. Isaiah states it dramatically: either the world of power and persecution, or the way of the God of Sinai. The early church stated it: either an antihuman world, or the way of Jesus—that is, the way of neighborly generosity and forgiveness. And so I state as clearly and dramatically as I am able that this contested question in our society must be seen in its largest scope. It must be said so that we are clear that we have choices to make between the dominant version of reality in our society and the sub-version that we believe carries the good news of God's love in the world.

There are two questions about this evangelical sub-version. The first one is whether it is true. In Isaiah it is proclaimed that the God of the Jews is the creator of heaven and earth who will finally decide about the affairs of nations and empires. The Jews had to ask, "Is it true that in the large reach of the Babylonian Empire there is a holy will for justice and well-being and mercy that will prevail?" In Luke it is asserted that the Friday/Sunday claim of Jesus is what the future of the world is about. That claim calls us to a freedom that the world cannot give and to a well-being that the world cannot take from us. And all these centuries, people around the church have been asking whether that is true. In our time, it is the claim of this sub-version that this God of Sinai and this Jesus of Nazareth have bent the world toward healing and well-being. Such a bending matters in the world of greenhouse effect and global economy and failed health care systems. So they asked the texts as you must ask these texts: is this true? Is it true, that "I am and there is no other," no other God, no other hope, no other future? Is it true so that it may be boldly contested in a way that is not gentle and accommodating? We ponder that riddle endlessly. If you are like me, on some days you say yes and on some days you mumble. We are here yet again to say yes as best we can.

The second question is, if it's true, is it worth it to embrace it and insist upon it and stand boldly in the heat of contest where these claims are so odd and so "sub" that we ourselves have a hard time with them? As you know, there are lots of reasons not to engage this sub-version of reality. It is too unproductive given the wholesale resistance of our society. It is too hard to oppose so dominant a version that is so powerful. And besides that, it doesn't do a lot of good. It is too demanding to go to court and enter always the contest when we only half believe it ourselves. The text in this matter of being witnesses is remarkable because it is a flat, uninflected indicative. The text says it is the word of God, "You are my witnesses." "You are my witnesses...and my servant whom I have chosen." One of the things you have to think about is that maybe you don't have a choice. Maybe that's an indicative about you. Then it goes on to say: "You are my witnesses"—get this—"so that you may know and believe me and understand that I am He." I thought that the purpose of testimony was to convince the others. This says that you are my witnesses in order that you may believe. You're supposed to talk yourselves into it. You're supposed to talk yourselves into it by talking about it. The purpose of the testimony is in order that the witnesses themselves may embrace this subversion of truth and so be free of the dominant version of reality that is a lie. The indicative is for our sake, so that we catch up with the truth of our own life.

Now I understand that is a circular argument. It's an argument that draws a conclusion from the premise. The only thing that goes beyond this circular reasoning is that the indicative is on the lips of the Holy One who speaks out from the foundation of creation about our true selves.

The indicatives are as flat in Luke as they are in Isaiah: "They will arrest you." Luke doesn't even say *maybe* they will arrest you. Well, in our society it means they may resent you. Luke says they will persecute you. Maybe they will just treat you unkindly. Luke says they will hand you over. Maybe they won't listen to you. And then Luke says, the good news is that that will give you the opportunity to go to court to testify. You'll get to meet the authorities. And then Jesus says— this is amazing—"Make up your minds not to prepare your defense in advance. Play it by ear. Wing it. Live your life in this sub-version and you'll know what to say when the time comes." And then Jesus says, "I will give you words." The Greek is amazing. Jesus says, "I will give you mouth." Well, probably some of you have too much mouth but that's a separate question. "I will give you wisdom for the truth that will be given in the moment of risk and contest." That's an offer, and the big question in your life is whether it is addressed to you.

Now, I have taken this rather odd approach with these texts because I believe that we are in an emergency situation in our society. There are people more urbane than I who do not believe that the emergency is so acute. But preaching, by design, is a place for dramatic overstatement. Preaching is a place for contested truth; I believe if Jews and Christians do not find ways to walk the walk and talk the talk credibly, then I think that the denial that precludes Friday and the despair that resists Sunday will continue to grind down our humanness into the power of death. You may not think it is that acute. But if you do think it's that acute, this might be for you. You want that again? If Jews and Christians do not find ways to walk the walk and talk the talk credibly, then I think that the denial that precludes Friday and the despair that resists Sunday will continue to grind down our humanness into the power of death. This either/or of walk and talk can take many forms. But every form is demanding and every form is risky. And every form is filled with great joy.

This is an odd assurance for people who are willing to enter the contest. Isaiah as God says to the witnesses, "Do not fear. Do not be afraid. Have I not told you and declared to you, you are my witnesses. Is there any God besides me? I know not one." Isn't it an amazing thing to say to a witness, "Don't be afraid"? I think it's not unlike an attorney saying, "Do not be afraid," to a woman who is about to testify in a rape trial. She would rather be anywhere else than on a witness stand and he says, "Do not be afraid." I think it's like an attorney speaking to a whistle-blower in a large corporation who's about to testify against the corporation and he would rather be anywhere else than on the witness stand and the attorney says, "Do not be afraid." The truth of the matter is that fear drives out real testimony, or even better, Luke says, "You will be hated by all because of my name. But not a hair on your head will perish. By your endurance you will gain your souls." Every hair on your head is made utterly safe because you have signed on to the truth that will sustain you.

The sub-version is a long shot. It's always been a long shot. But the question about this vocation does not finally concern poor pay or the fact that there are a lot of recalcitrant people in the church or the fact that the church itself is a frozen institution or that you miss out on a lot of power if you do this. The only real question is whether people like us can stay in the contests of testimony. This sub-version insists that the eternal truth of the Holy God is linked to the full humanness of the world and the full abundance of creation. Everything turns on that linkage between the Holy God and the well-being of the world. And if there is not a decisive connection, then it is better to sign on with the dominant version with its little pockets of well-being for privileged people like us. So I assume, no matter what you do you will be like me: you will always be deciding this. Our deciding is set between an indicative, "You are my witness," and an assurance, "Do not fear." That's all: you are my witness, do not fear. It's a very thin place for this sub-version. But the truth of it is that it is thick with joy and deep with well-being, and the court is in session.

# In the Lord's House, on the Lord's Day

## Jeremiah A. Wright, Jr.

*Again he entered the synagogue, and a man was there who had a withered hand. They watched him to see whether he would cure him on the sabbath, so that they might accuse him. And he said to the man who had the withered hand, "Come forward." Then he said to them, "Is it lawful to do good or to do harm on the sabbath, to save a life or to kill?" But they were silent. He looked around at them with anger; he was grieved at their hardness of heart and said to the man, "Stretch out your hand." He stretched it out, and his hand was restored. The Pharisees went out and immediately conspired with the Herodians against him, how to destroy him.*

—Mark 3:1-6

Mark 3, verse 1 says, "Again he entered the synagogue, and a man was there who had a withered hand. They watched him to see whether he would cure him on the sabbath."

"Again he entered the synagogue." That first sentence in Mark 3 has enough explosive material in it to preach an entire series of sermons. That first verse in Mark 3 has enough inspiration in it to help somebody make it through another week.

That first picture painted by the opening words of Mark 3 has enough truth in it to make somebody start to shout.

Just think about what the word of God is saying in fifteen short words. Start, if you will, with just the first word: "Again." *Again!* Again means that this is not the first time the Lord has done this. *Again.*

"Again" means that this is no new activity, no new behavior, no new exercise in spirituality. "Again" means Jesus had already been where he was going. "Again" means he'd already engaged in what he was engaging in in this passage. "Again" means Jesus knew something about being in the Lord's house on the Lord's day. The text says, "*Again* he entered the synagogue."

Jesus knew what a lot of us already know and Jesus knew what a lot of men need to know. Jesus knew that being in the Lord's house on the Lord's day does something for your soul and does something for your spirit that a six-pack can't do, that sex can't do, that sports can't do, that parties can't do, that the fraternity can't do. Nothing else can do what this experience can do for you.

There is something about hearing the songs of Zion in the Lord's house on the Lord's day that does something to you that is almost indescribable. You can turn on gospel radio and hear those same songs. You can buy a tape or CD and play those same songs. You can do what I do and go get you a Richard Smallwood *Live in Atlanta* video and watch and enjoy those same songs.

But neither radio, tape, CD, nor video can touch that spiritual nerve, way down deep on the inside like being in the Lord's house on the Lord's day can touch it. There's something about mingling my voice with the other voices in the house of God. Something about hearing the music in this kind of a setting.

You know, some songs you can sing by yourself. As a matter of fact some of you try to sing them by yourself—in the shower, driving down the street. But there are some other songs that cannot be sung all by yourself. In the 1800s there was a genre of music that came about when it was against the law to teach Africans how to read.

And because the Africans were not allowed to learn how to read, one person would sing out a line of a hymn and the congregation would answer. It is called common meter singing. And see, you can't—and if you know it, I need you to help me—you can't sing this kind of song by yourself. When I sing, "I love the Lord, He heard my cry," the congregation sings, "I love the Lord, He heard my cry." You can't do that by yourself, it's got to be in a communal or congregational setting.

One of my friends has been flirting with the theology and the sociology of another religion for several years now. He says that the teachings of self-pride and self-worth make him conscious of how important it is to be a black man of dignity and integrity. He says that the teaching of support for your own black businesses and support for your own black professionals make him conscious of the need for self-determination, self-definition, and self-affirmation. And he's right! I mean, it's time out from thinking that other people are superior to your own people. My friend says he's sick and tired of Negro preachers who want to be white and Negro preachers who want to be rich and Negro preachers who don't want to be black. I have a lot of black preachers asking me, "Why we always gotta be talking about that black stuff?"

He says that he needs the teaching of self-pride and self-worth. He needs the teaching of black integrity and dignity. He needs the practice and support of his own businesses and his own professionals. And he keeps arguing with me. He's a doctor. He says, "I tell you, I am sick and tired of black folk driving past my office, no *running* past or jumping *over* my office to get to a white doctor. 'Cause there ain't no white folk coming in from the suburbs to my black office in the black 'hood." And he says he needs what this other religion can give, because they are honest and they deal with reality.

But over the ten years we've been arguing about this matter (for ten years!) he keeps on hanging around the church. He reads the books of this other religion, but he keeps hanging around our church. We have three services on Sunday. Seven thirty in the morning, eleven and six at night. Every Sunday night when I look up in the balcony, there is brother man, my doctor friend, praising God.

And when I ask him how come he doesn't just cut us loose, he says, "There's just something about hearing the music *in this setting*. Hearing songs that my mamma used to sing. Songs that bring tears to my eyes, songs that remind of a love that is stronger than hate, a God who is mightier than our mess, and a transcendence that transforms the trash of our society. There's just something about being in the Lord's house on the Lord's day that feeds my spirit like nothing else can."

So the text says, "Again." Again, Jesus has his feet on the path leading him into the Lord's house. How did David put it? "I was glad when they said unto me, 'Let us go into the house of the Lord.' " Again, says Mark, again, Jesus is going into the Lord's house. This was a man who is all man going into the presence of the Lord to reconnect, to hook back up with the Holy. *Again* he was going to sing. *Again* he was going to pray. *Again* he was going to listen. *Again* he was going to be fed.

And verse 1 says, "A man was there who had a withered hand." I love this verse. I'm telling you, there's more in this one sentence than you can fit in any one sermon. Look at it—a man with a withered hand. Look at him—a man with a serious problem. Look at him—a man with a situation that seemed unsolvable. Look at him—a man with a condition that was not going to change. Look at him—a man with something wrong with him that everybody knew about.

You know, a whole lot of us have things wrong with us—now wait a minute—I'm saying that the wrong way. Somebody's going to miss it. Let me put it another way: *everybody's* got something wrong with them.

Everybody's got something going on in their lives. Everybody has some area where they need a little work. Everybody has something wrong with them. Some of us have stuff that's wrong with us that we can keep hidden. We got stuff—what is that psychological word they're using now? Issues! We've got issues!

We've got issues that other folk don't know anything at all about. We can keep our stuff away from the public eye. That is what *some* of us can do. But then, there are others of us, and we've got stuff going on in our lives that *everybody* knows about.

Some of us have stuff that everybody can see. Others of us have stuff that we keep hidden. This man in Mark 3 had stuff in his life that everybody knew about. The man has something wrong with him that was public knowledge. This man, as a matter of fact, look at the text—Mark doesn't even call the man's name. The only reason he made the holy record was because he had something wrong with him that everybody knew about.

The only reason this story gets in here is because of his "stuff"—his issues! He was known as "the man with the withered hand." You know him, don't you? I mean, if his hand hadn't been withered, wouldn't nobody have noticed him! He would not have stood out in a crowd. You know him, don't you?

He was the man with a withered hand. He was the man who had something wrong with him. He was the man who lost his wife to another man. He was the man who could not hold his marriage together. He was the man who was always out of work. He was the man who had children out of wedlock. He was the man who was married to one woman and had a baby by some other woman. You know him, don't you?

Don't you know her? The woman—you know, she's the girl who got pregnant by the married man. Everybody knows her stuff. She was the girl who got married—she had no more business getting married than I have being a brain surgeon. You know her! Everybody knows her "stuff."

She was the one over there in John 8 who got caught in the very act of adultery. Everybody knows her stuff. She used to be on drugs—I think I saw her on the Jerry Springer show! I mean, you know her, don't you? Everybody knows about her!

Everybody knows him—he is the man with the withered hand. He doesn't have it all together. He is the man who is HIV positive. He is the man with the unchangeable situation in his life. He is the man who is forever marked by something over which he had no control. And everybody sits around speculating, who did what to make him end up the way he is? He is the man with the withered hand. You know him. He's the one with something wrong with him that everybody knows about.

But look at the text one more time, and look, if you will, at where he is. He is in the Lord's house on the Lord's day. Look what the text is teaching us: you don't let what's going on in your life, you don't let whatever is wrong with you keep you from coming into the Lord's house on the Lord's day. You don't let whatever your situation is, you don't let "stuff" that can't be changed, you don't let situations over which you have no control, you don't let your issues, you don't let things that everybody knows about, situations that everybody is talking about, stuff that everybody can see, and everybody's got an opinion about, you don't let public opinion or personal pain keep you from coming to the Lord's house on the Lord's day.

Here is the one place where you can get from God just what you need. Here in the Lord's house is the one place where you can get from on high what you need to make it down low. This is the one place where God can give you what the world can't give you and God can give you what the world can't take away. In the Lord's house on the Lord's day. You can get your soul fed. You can get your spirit led. You can get your hope restored. You can get your faith renewed.

The song says, "Here, bring your wounded heart." Here, you can tell Jesus all of your troubles. Here you can kneel at the altar and pray to a God who will meet you at the point of need. Here you will find joy that's unspeakable, love that's unconditional and grace that is still sufficient. So you don't let what's going on in your life keep you away from the house of Him who gave you your life. Who cares what other folks know and what other people say? You're not coming here to worship them; you're coming to worship Him!

Look at the text. Brother man came to worship with his withered hand and all. He came to worship. Unchangeable circumstances were in his life. He came to worship. Stuff was going on over which he had no control. He came to worship. A painful situation that everybody knew about and most folks probably talked about. He came to worship.

He did not let his human pain keep him away from God's holy power. He came to worship. If you could just learn that one lesson from this text, it would make a major difference in your life. You don't let what's going on in your personal life keep you away from the Lord's house on the Lord's day. You come and worship the Lord.

He promised to meet you here. He said, "where two or three are gathered," so you come and worship. It's no concern of yours why other folk come. You come and worship.

I wonder, do we have any worshipers here this afternoon? "This is the day that the Lord has made, let us rejoice and be glad in it." The man with the withered hand came to the Lord's house to worship, on the Lord's day. And he's about to be blessed beyond his wildest dreams. Think about it—folks back home are not going to recognize him because of what the Lord is getting ready to do for him.

And don't you know that the Lord will change you? The Lord will change you so that the folks you left at home won't recognize you once you get back home. If you come into His presence and you hook up with him on the Lord's day, you watch out. You'll go home a different way. You'll go out of the Lord's house a different person than when you came into the Lord's house. The man came to worship and the Lord blessed him like never before.

But look, wait a minute. If you've got your Bible, open it back up, because before you can get to the blessing, if you look at the text, the very next thing you will see—before you can get to the blessing you will see some "blessing blockers."

Verse 2 says, "They"—the first word, "they." Who is "they"? Blessing blockers. They watch Jesus to see whether he would cure him on the Sabbath. Stop right there. Look at what the text is saying. There are some folk in the Lord's house on the Lord's day who are in the right place. But they are in the right place for all the wrong reasons. They didn't come to worship. Look at verse 2, they came to watch.

Some folk can't worship because they are too busy watching. You'll hear them and see them at your church. Sometimes you'll sit on the same pew with them. They'll be saying things like, "Look, look, look, look. See who she's sitting next to? OK, OK?" Watching.

"Look at what Reverend's got on today. I wonder when his old lady gonna buy him some new shoes." You can't concentrate on *Him* for watching *them*. You can't worship for watching. The text says, "They watched him."

Everybody in the right place ain't in the right place for the right reasons. Some folk come with scorn on their agenda. They're watching. Some come with sarcasm on their agenda. They're watching instead of worshiping. Did you come to watch this afternoon, or did you come to worship?

Some folk, the years have taught me, can't worship God because they are too busy watching people. And there are other folk who can't worship God because they are self-conscious about who is watching them. And let me tell you something, in case you haven't found out. You can't be cute and praise God.

To praise God, you are going to get ugly. Don't you let the watchers stop you from worshiping. Those who came to watch have one agenda and one agenda only: blocking blessings. Jesus wants to bless and they want to block. They don't want you to get what the Lord has in store for you. They don't want you to have what the Lord has to give you.

They are miserable and they want you to be miserable with them. Blessing blockers, I call them. You know the blessing blockers, don't you? Them the folk who don't never smile. Blessing blockers sit up in the church like it's a séance. Folk be up on their feet praising God, worshiping the Lord, lifting holy hands and the blessing blockers, man, they're trying to block your blessings and they are blocking their own blessings in the process.

You know the blessing blockers, don't you? They're not there to worship. They're there to watch. Somebody shouts over here and instead of giving God the glory, they watch. Somebody starts praising God over here and instead of thanking God, they watch. Something goes on up in the balcony and instead of saying, "Thank you God for a breakthrough, thank you for a burden that's been lifted," they turn around to watch.

You know the blessing blockers, don't you? They're always critical. They can always find some fault with the service. "That second song was too long. Why we got to sing all four verses of that thing?" They *always* find some fault. When some of my preachers I invite to the church preach, they say their sermons were too long. When I preach they say the sermon was too short. I've had people tell me this, "Reverend, just when I was getting ready to shout, you cut it off." And I say, "You don't shout because of what I say, you shout because of what the Lord has done in your life." There's a song we sing in our church that says, "When I think about Jesus…" It doesn't say, "When I think about Jerry and what he said to me." It says, "When I think about Jesus and what he's done for me." That's why you shout—because of what Jesus has done.

But if you'll notice, the man with the withered hand doesn't let the blessing blockers keep him from getting the blessing that the Lord has to give. Look at it. Look! It says—Jesus said, "Come forward," and the man came forward. The man listened to Jesus, not to the blessing blockers. When he said, "Come forward," he came forward. When Jesus said, "Stretch out your hand," he stretched out his hand.

Has the Lord called you? Can you respond to that call? Do you have a relationship with the Lord, or as in my tradition, they say, "Do you know him for yourself?" Can you respond like this man—out of faith? Can you come forward when he calls you?

Let me tell you how it came alive for me. I spent six years at the University of Chicago Divinity School in the Ph.D. program of the History of Religion. Now the University of Chicago Divinity School—most people don't know this—is a Baptist school.

And so, what they would do years ago when I was there, they would have "Baptist Day" once a year. They would invite all the Baptist ministers in the city to come up on the campus and spend a day hearing lectures from Old Testament, New Testament, theologians, scholars, historians of religion, ethicists, and church historians. And they would have a sack lunch. Sack lunch means you bring your own lunch in a brown paper bag and you drink that same red punch that I just saw y'all drinking: saved, sanctified pink punch that they serve in every church.

They provide the punch and you bring your sack lunch. Well, this particular day, I think it was my third year there,

1972, one of the lecturers lectured for two hours—one hour and fifty-seven minutes I think it was—lecturing on the fact that there was no such thing as the resurrection of Jesus. Hugh Schoenfeld had written a book, *The Passover Plot*, about those "incredible Christians," trying to show that it was all a conspiracy to keep hope alive. The scholar demonstrated that the disciples of Jesus, as it says in Matthew, moved the body, but there was no actual resurrection. Jesus did not get up from the dead. He was a good guy, but he did not rise from the dead.

He quoted the texts from Qumran, the Dead Sea Scrolls. He quoted Schleiermacher. He quoted Nietzsche—oh, he was quoting every source he could to buttress his major premise, and when he finished he said, "Are there any questions?" For forty seconds it was dead silence in that room. You could hear a rat urinating on cotton at a hundred yards. And finally one of the black preachers sitting in the back of Swift Hall 104 stood up and he said, "Yeah, Doc, I got a question for you."

He reached into his sack lunch and pulled out an apple. "My question is—*crunch*," and he bit the apple, "I have not been to Qumran, and I can't read those languages—*crunch*— you were talking about. I went to school here. I know some Schleiermacher—*crunch*—and some Hegel and Nietzsche— *crunch*—and them boys are all right, but here's my question, *crunch, crunch, crunch*. My question is, *Was the apple I just ate bitter, or was it sweet?*"

And the professor said, "Sir, I don't have any empirical evidence by which to measure such an interrogatory. I cannot possibly answer that question. I did not taste the apple. You did." And the old preacher said, "Well, that's what I wanted to tell you about my Jesus. 'O taste and see that the Lord is good!' I tried him for myself. I know him for myself. And he's sweet—I know. I have a personal relationship with him. Boy, you need to meet the Lord Jesus for yourself!"

Therein, my brothers and my sisters, is what makes the difference in your ministry and your call to ministry. You can't get up preaching what Schleiermacher said, what Tillich said, what Bultmann said. Jesus said, *"You* shall be my witnesses." You gotta talk about your relationship with the Lord, what the Lord has done in your life. What you know the Lord has done. "I have found a Savior, and He is sweet, I know."